well being

well being

REJUVENATING RECIPES *for* BODY AND SOUL

by BARBARA CLOSE

photographs by SUSIE CUSHNER

CHRONICLE BOOKS

SAN FRANCISCO

Library of Congress Cataloging-in-Publication Data available.
ISBN 0-8118-2593-0

Printed in Hong Kong.

Styled by JACQUELINE LEMIEUX-BOKOR
Designed by SARA SCHNEIDER

The photographer wishes to extend sincere thanks to:
Jacqueline Lemieux-Bokor; Michael Carabetta; Sara Schneider; Barbara Close; Charlene Engelhard; Barbara Bourgault; the Washburn family; Gregory and Quinn Bokor; Jenna and Kayla Cushner; Nola Anderson and James X. Mullen; Eliza Lloyd; Alison Kuller; Cathy Sullivan; Roland, Mary, and Annette Lemieux; Ginger Dreier; Marston House; Cricket Hill Herb Farm; Goodale Orchards; and Sedgwick Gardens, a property of The Trustees of Reservations.

This book owes a great deal to the spirit and dedication of my creative collaborator and friend Jacqueline Lemieux-Bokor.

Distributed in Canada by Raincoast Books
8680 Cambie Street
Vancouver, British Columbia V6P 6M9

10 9 8 7 6 5 4 3 2 1

Chronicle Books
85 Second Street
San Francisco, California 94105
www.chroniclebooks.com

FDA DISCLAIMER
These herbal remedies have not been evaluated by the Food and Drug Administration and are not intended to diagnose, cure, mitigate, treat, or prevent disease. The author is not responsible for any effects or consequences that may result from the use of these remedies. The remedies are created from traditional sources of herbal knowledge.

DEDICATION

To my mother, whose love of the plant world was my inspiration.

ACKNOWLEDGMENTS: I am deeply appreciative of the many people who helped give shape to this book. My father, whose unwavering love has always provided me with strength. My sisters, Louise and Kate, for their guidance and my brother, Peter, who courageously showed me that humor and a positive outlook are instrumental to the healing path.

My gratitude also goes to Ed Herbst and Alicia Ziecina for their unending patience and support. Lorin Parish, head of the New Mexico Academy of Healing Arts, whose dedication toward promoting good health helped shape my vision. Sherry Houck, a true healer, teacher, and friend, who was generous enough to share her wisdom. Mark Thompson, friend and author, whose critical encouragement was invaluable. Martha Rose Shulman, cooking expert and author, generously donated her time and culinary talents to provide recipes for this book. And finally, Jacqueline Becker, whose musical talents always help to turn my sad songs of woe into Gershwin melodies.

I would also like to thank all those whose unpremeditated kindness meant so much to me: Rosanne and Steve Nenninger, Cris and Nanette at Peconic River Herb Farm, Susie Cushner and Jacqueline Lemieux-Bokor for being "my eyes," and all the staff at Naturopathica. Special thanks to Leslie Jonath, Mikyla Bruder, and Michael Carabetta at Chronicle Books for their guidance.

Finally, my gratitude to the great long lineage of natural health practitioners whose unwavering commitment to healing with medicines out of the earth has given us invaluable healing lessons.

CONTENTS

INTRODUCTION

The best remedies for our ills are often the simplest.

The honeylike scent of freshly picked chamomile flowers wafting above a cup of hot tea and the healing touch of a partner's hand on a stiff shoulder offer sensual as well as therapeutic awards. Consider the relaxation of taking a bath. The faucet turns reluctantly. There is a pause followed by a rising hum and finally water gushes forth. A quick swish of the hand in the water, then one foot, followed by the other. You ease back against the porcelain embrace of the tub and exhale deeply. Steam rises with vapors of freshly picked lavender and clary sage to quiet your senses while the measured drips from the tap slow your mind. The ritual of the bath allows the healing waters to restore the mind, body, and spirit, and you emerge renewed. Such rituals comfort and soothe while supporting the body's own innate ability to heal.

All of us at some point in our lives will have to embark upon a healing path. Before the advent of modern medicine with high-tech diagnostics and synthetic mass-produced drugs, people harvested herbs and relied upon experiential knowledge of natural remedies to maintain and restore their health. This relationship with natural therapies was not only effective; it was pleasurable and empowering since it made individuals active participants in their recovery.

The resurgence of interest in natural health has caused the scientific community to look eagerly for grants to validate the effectiveness of treatments such as meditation and aromatherapy. But attempting to scientifically validate these healing arts in reductionist terms, while perhaps useful, does not completely explain the full spectrum of healing. Many of us know someone with some sort of chronic ailment—migraines, eczema, or stomach problems—who was prescribed drugs by doctors to no avail. But after making lifestyle changes to create healthy work habits, substitute herbal teas for caffeine, take up yoga classes, or schedule weekly aromatherapy massage appointments—all scientifically unproved—they were able to completely free themselves of their ailment.

Well Being is a self-care manual to enhance your body's ability to heal itself and to reawaken your senses to the rewarding rituals of natural healing. What is missing in our depersonalized health care today is a deeper response to illness than advanced technology can provide. Our most important work comes between visits to the doctor when we learn to listen to and respect our body's cues rather than override them. Sound health is not defined as the absence of disease. Rather, symptoms are messengers our body sends us as opportunities for change. The recipes in this book will help you to use and enjoy the benefits of aromatherapy, herbalism, meditation, massage, and hydrotherapy to function optimally.

If we take the time to care for ourselves preventively, instead of automatically turning to an external authority of doctors, media experts, or gurus to prescribe our healing path, we gain insight and understanding of who we are. This concept frees us from suppressing our symptoms as in modern Western medicine or depriving or punishing ourselves as with some forms of alternative medicine. At times, it seems that alternative therapies look the same as Western allopathic medicine because consumers approach treatment with a similar "quick fix" mind-set—they apply Herculean measures in an attempt to solve their problems. Punishing dietary regimens such as raw juice fasting, invasive measures such as colon therapy, excessive exercise routines, or an overzealous intake of the latest dietary supplements do not measure up to vibrant health.

At my holistic health center, Naturopathica, I often see clients who wish to more fully understand their illness and want to learn a broader holistic approach to health that does not just treat the symptoms. The first step toward building optimum health is to learn to be a better observer. If chronic headaches are a problem for you, instead of just taking painkillers, focus on why these headaches happen. Perhaps it is your body's way of telling you to slow down. When you eat certain foods, do they make you feel energized or lethargic? Does jogging make you feel depleted rather than refreshed? Being healthy is about honoring the spirit of your being and having the willingness and discipline to give your body what it needs. Chapter One lays the foundation for cultivating this awareness.

The following pages are designed to enable you to be an active participant in your own health care. You will find simple recipes for fortifying herbal beverages; aromatic massage and bath oils and botanical body care treatments as well as remedies for specific ailments. Each recipe focuses on nurturing and supporting your body in a fun and spontaneous way throughout the year. The chapter for the spring season concentrates on renewal by exploring delicious herbal drinks and effective botanical treatments to strengthen your body and combat the effects of stress and fatigue. Many natural healers see the beginning of the year as the optimum time to cleanse and renew the body; you will find recipes that address this topic as well. In summertime, the verdant outdoors allows you to replenish your body with fresh herbal and floral remedies from the garden. This chapter suggests what to plant in your own medicinal herb garden or window box and then demonstrates how to take advantage of those restorative ingredients to nurture your body. The chapter for the autumn months focuses on preparing for cooling temperatures, shorter days, and the colder, darker months ahead. By stocking the herbal remedy chest with homemade herbal oils and balms you can have a ready supply of materials to treat a variety of ailments. With the arrival of winter, keeping your strength and vitality becomes paramount. The winter chapter features nutritive tonics, teas, and soups as well as immune-enhancing treatments to keep you strong.

These treatments, founded upon some of the oldest medical traditions, bring the pleasure, warmth, and simplicity back into caring for yourself. When life becomes a whirl and you begin to feel that you are losing your equilibrium, these rewarding rituals will restore the balance between mind and body.

A FOUNDATION
for HEALTH

1

A FOUNDATION *for* HEALTH

Like everyone else, I look forward to time off and the chance to unwind.

On about the fifth day into a recent vacation I noticed a subtle shift in how my body felt. I woke up and realized that not only did I feel rested, but the chronic pain and tension in my lower back had disappeared. As the day progressed I found that my anger at the small things—an interruption or a misplaced set of keys—had abated. Away from the day-to-day hassles of everyday life, my mental, emotional, and physical self was reawakened and I felt fresh to become reacquainted with my more balanced self.

Losing touch with ourselves is easy to do these days. We are conditioned to ignore the warning signs that protect us from becoming ill. Instead we push ahead to meet deadlines and live up to our responsibilities and commitments until fatigue or sickness overwhelms us and forces us to stop.

For much of our lives we live on automatic pilot, living day to day without consciously engaging ourselves. Instead of focusing on the present moment, we focus on the past or where we want to go in the future and are only vaguely aware of our inner tension. We may find ourselves intensely reading the back of a cereal box and before we realize it, we have hastily eaten three bowls of cereal. By not paying close attention to this dynamic, we unconsciously commit ourselves to a deep spiritual impoverishment. We shortchange ourselves of our full potential.

Self-awareness is a prerequisite for good health. By deepening our attention we can be more in tune with our bodies and freed from the constant stream of thoughts that pull us away from the deeper, richer part of ourselves. The reward for this attention is a recovered connection to our own wisdom and sense of purpose. This concept of living more fully in the present is at the heart of Buddhist and Taoist philosophy.

Meditation is a process to help us deepen our attention and get in touch with our true selves. This is especially difficult in our fast-paced, consumer-oriented world. When I was first introduced to meditation during an introductory seminar, I struggled to cope with strict rules about posture and breath. I assumed meditation had to be a rigid discipline that required me to get up each day at sunrise, to sit erect and perfectly still for forty-five minutes in order to achieve the benefits. Armed with my newly acquired skills and unbridled optimism, I started my meditation practice when I returned home. On my first day, I rose at 5:30 in the morning, lit some votive candles, and put on a CD of Tibetan monks' chanting that I am sure forever changed my relationship with my neighbors. I sat upright on the floor, took deep, full breaths, and tried to focus on nothing. It was horrible. Unable to focus on the present moment, I was in agony. My knees ached and, even worse, my mind was like a superball in a marble hallway. I gave up after thirty minutes.

Some people get discouraged with meditation because they think they are supposed to adhere to strict spiritual guidelines in order to attain some form of elusive "enlightenment." Meditation is simply a tool for connecting with your true self and does not have to be a rigid form of practice for you to benefit from it. Learning to focus your attention is rigorous work and you have to be ready to listen to your intuition. Posture and breath are important building blocks to assist you in disciplining the mind, but don't let them discourage you at the outset. Once you learn to focus your mind, meditation can be done while preparing a meal, doing the dishes, or walking the dog.

Begin your meditation practice by keeping it simple. All you have to do is be present. Sit still and be aware of your breath. Breathe and let go. In and out. You can try a mantra if you want but the best way is to focus on your breath. The involuntary rhythm of breathing acts like a metronome with which to focus our attention. Just feel the breath coming in and going out.

Next, be an observer. Don't try to think or feel anything. Most important, don't try to achieve results. The beauty of meditation is that it is the one place in our lives where we can allow ourselves not to have an outcome. Just fully experience the moment. You can only do that by simply being present and observing what comes up inside of you.

When you begin a meditation, the process can be much like a press conference. Thoughts and feelings come rushing forward for attention. Acknowledge them and try to let them go. You don't have to act on those thoughts. It is difficult not to let yourself be captured by your thoughts and become unaware again. The mind is used to jumping from one idea to the next; it is humbling to realize how scattered and fragmented one's mind is most of the time. If you can wait it out long enough for the mind to settle down, gradually you will develop increased periods of awareness. Finally, a calm emerges and you can relax in just being present, nothing more, and fully savor the moment. Crossing this gateway empowers you to reconnect with your inner resources of creativity and intuition. This can transform your outer world in healthy and compassionate ways.

There is no one right way to meditate. Try to set aside thirty minutes a day for your practice. This is usually enough time to get through your random thoughts and ease into stillness. But certainly twenty minutes, or ten or five minutes will reward you. If you cannot sit erect like a mountain then use pillows or lie down and get comfortable. The most important thing is that you try with the best of your intention. Feel good about your endeavor and feel the pulse of each and every moment.

the HERBAL REMEDY CHEST

Everyone should have an herbal remedy chest in the home.

Before the rise of modern pharmaceuticals in the earlier 1900s, herbal medicine was the predominant form of health care, and the kitchen of every home was also an apothecary. Many of us have lost touch with a safe and effective form of healing; modern medicine has divorced us from the sensual pleasure daily herbal self-care techniques provide.

Modern medicine had its origins, of course, in herbalism. Prescription drugs and over-the-counter medications are made synthetically by isolating the medicinally active ingredients from plants and then synthesizing them, as in the case of salicin, the active ingredient in aspirin—derived from willow bark. These medicines tend to be much more aggressive than their natural counterparts because they lack the synergistic action of all the ingredients that nature provides to balance the effectiveness of an herb. Hippocrates wrote that the first rule of medicine was to "cause no harm." Yet the side effects of many mainstream medicines often outweigh the benefits.

Not to disregard the role modern medicine plays in our lives: it has its place. But with chronic illness we must take care not to indulge in the convenience of pills and quick fixes that often help to mask our symptoms, instead of listening to our bodies. What is often missing from the modern attitude toward health is that we are responsible for our well-being rather than relying solely on an external authority. With chronic illnesses, not only is the individual the best judge of what symptoms represent but usually the cure lies in taking one's own steps to help the body better cure itself.

As an herbalist interested in medicine with vitality, I prefer to make my own preparations from fresh herbs. This assures me of quality: the less processed an herb is, the more effective it will be. Just as with food, the more processed an herb is, the more stress it puts on the body's organs and the harder it is for the body to absorb it effectively. This is a challenge in terms of convenience, but the process of collecting herbs, brewing teas, or custom blending an oil will revitalize your senses and provide a wonderful feeling of self-sufficiency.

On the following pages, guidelines are given for creating remedies using herbs and essential oils to treat everyday ailments. To list every therapeutic herb and essential oil available as a healing agent is beyond the scope of this book. Highlighting a selection of herbs and essential oils to enhance your health regimen, these remedies will become the building blocks for you and your family to create simple rituals for health and wellness throughout the year.

HERBAL MEDICINE

The herbal supplement industry is exploding, and it has become difficult for the consumer to sort through the maze of conflicting information. It is disheartening to see health food store clerks prescribe remedies to people who have just walked in off the street; just because an herb is natural does not necessarily mean it is safe. If you are unfamiliar with herbs you should consult a qualified specialist such as a naturopath or herbalist who can recommend your treatment. Many physicians are gaining familiarity with herbal products, so do not be afraid to tell your doctor that you are taking botanicals. This is especially important if you are taking prescription drugs since herbs can sometimes alter their effects.

Herbs contain hundreds of biochemical constituents that have therapeutic effects on the body. For example, the tannins found in an herb give it an astringent quality. Some of the properties herbs contain are alteratives (cleansing the bloodstream and toning organs), adaptogens (producing a normalizing effect on the body), analgesics, antacids, antibiotics, antiseptics, antispasmodics, and diaphoretics (inducing perspiration), to name a few.

A number of plants are quite safe and effective and would be a valuable ally to have in your herbal remedy chest. These herbs are safe to use both internally and externally to maintain your health and to treat a variety of conditions. Growing, harvesting, and preparing your own herbal remedies can be fun and satisfying to do but many people have time constraints that make this impossible. In this section you will find techniques to make your own herbal preparations from scratch, or you can consult the Resources section in the back of this book to find ready-made material to stock your herbal medicine cabinet.

If you do not have time to grow and collect your own herbs, make sure to purchase your herbs from a reliable source, one that guarantees they have not been sprayed with pesticides or otherwise contaminated. In general, the loose bulk herbs that you find in bins at the health food store are lacking in value. You never know how long the herb has been sitting there, and most of the active ingredients have probably dwindled due to exposure to light and air. The same is true for powdered dried herbs in capsule form. Herbal capsules often contain binders and fillers, nonessential ingredients that diminish the ability of the body to absorb the active ingredients of the herb. If you do want to work with dried herbs, be sure to buy them from a reputable supplier (see the Resources section). Dried herbs should be brightly colored, fresh smelling, and as whole as possible.

An easy and effective way to ingest an herbal remedy when dried or fresh herbs are not available is in a liquid extract form, called a tincture. Tinctures are available at most health food stores. A tincture is prepared by steeping herbs in alcohol for four to six weeks; the herb is then strained off and the active constituents are preserved. The amount of alcohol is small; you can opt to buy tinctures in a glycerin base instead. Tinctures usually come in 1-ounce bottles with droppers. A typical dose is 15 to 30 drops every two hours for acute symptoms and 15 to 30 drops four times a day for chronic symptoms. You can add them to water or tea—or to juice since herbs can be bitter tasting.

Special precautions:
Always exercise caution with herbs. If you experience an adverse reaction, discontinue use immediately. Since herbs react differently for each individual, listen to the messages your body is giving you and adjust the dosage accordingly. Keep in mind that most herbs work much more slowly than modern synthesized medicines. It usually takes two to three weeks for an herb to have an effect on the body unless the herb is an immune system activator, in which case it will take effect more quickly. Stop taking an herb when symptoms cease.

THE HERBAL FIRST AID KIT

The following herbs are all safe in moderation and easy to use to support your body on its healing paths. The entries listed below correspond to the herbs pictured on the previous pages.

HERB	PROPERTIES
A} **ARNICA** (*Arnica montana*): The flower tops of this herb are well known for treating rheumatism or sprains.	anti-inflammatory
B} **BURDOCK** (*Arctium lappa*): The roots of this common field green are full of nutritive value.	alterative, diuretic, tonic
C} **CALENDULA** (*Calendula officinalis*): Commonly known as pot marigold, the flower heads of this plant are a traditional remedy for treating skin complaints.	anti-inflammatory, astringent
D} **DANDELION** (*Taraxacum officinalis*): The roots and leaves of this valuable, nutritious herb are used internally for their tonifying benefits.	diuretic, liver tonic
E} **ECHINACEA** (*Echinacea purpurea*): The roots and leaves of this traditional Native American remedy are an important immune system stimulant. Good-quality echinacea, when ingested, produces a slight tingling sensation on your tongue.	antibiotic, alterative
F} **GINGER** (*Zingiber officinalis*): Esteemed in Asian countries for its stimulating properties, this root is important for promoting perspiration and calming digestive upset.	diaphoretic, stimulant

COMMON USES

Used externally on unbroken skin, arnica is one of the most popular remedies to reduce inflammation for sore muscles, bruises, and sprains. Infuse arnica in a carrier oil such as olive oil or safflower oil and apply to affected area.

Used internally as a nourishing tonic, burdock is an excellent blood purifier and has high iron and mineral content. Excellent remedy for skin complaints such as eczema and psoriasis.

Ideal external first aid treatment for minor burns or inflammation of the skin. Use as a salve or infused oil.

Take internally for an effective liver tonic; the leaves act as a diuretic for water retention.

Take internally to boost your immune system at the first sign of cold or flu, or to support the lymphatic system in reducing inflammation.

Drink as tea to ward off colds and flu or to ease nausea and gastric disturbances.

CAUTION

Do not take internally.

Use in moderation. Pregnant women should avoid burdock root.

HERB	PROPERTIES
G} **AMERICAN GINSENG** *(Panax quinquefolium)*: Milder than Siberian ginseng, this form of ginseng helps boost the immune system, especially when recovering from illness.	adaptogen, antibiotic
H} **SIBERIAN GINSENG** *(Eleutherococcus senticosus)*: The root of this herb is a well-known stimulant to increase endurance and to combat stress.	adaptogen, stimulant, tonic
I} **KAVA KAVA** *(Piper methysticum)*: The root of this herb, indigenous to the South Pacific, calms the mind and sedates the body.	antispasmodic, relaxant
J} **LEMON BALM** *(Melissa officinalis)*: A gentle herb with a delicious lemon mint flavor.	sedative, antispasmodic
K} **LICORICE ROOT** *(Glycyrrhiza glabra)*: A soothing relaxant herb with sweet taste.	anti-inflammatory, sedative, expectorant, laxative
L} **RED CLOVER** *(Trifolium pratense)*: The flowers of this common backyard plant are a powerful blood cleanser and may have antitumor compounds.	alterative, tonic
M} **SAINT JOHN'S WORT** *(Hypericum perforatum)*: A popular herb taken internally for treating depression and soothing neuralgia, this plant is also useful applied externally to help dry skin conditions.	antidepressant, anti-inflammatory, sedative, analgesic
N} **SKULLCAP** *(Scutellaria lateriflora)*: A nervous system relaxant valuable for stress-related conditions.	sedative, antispasmodic, nervous system relaxant
O} **VALERIAN** *(Valeriana officinalis)*: A strong sedative (unrelated to the drug Valium) to assist with sleeping disorders.	sedative, hypnotic, antispasmodic, nervous system relaxant

COMMON USES

Take this fortifying herb to increase resistance to infection.

Use this tonifying herb internally to increase your stamina.

Drink as tea to relieve stress-related symptoms.

Drink tea made from the leaves to calm digestive disorders or to ease nervous tension.

Drink tea made from the roots to support adrenal function.

Valuable taken internally for its immune system enhancing properties as well as a soothing remedy for skin ailments.

Take internally to treat mild depression or ease nerve pain, or apply externally as an infused oil to treat eczema, psoriasis, or dermatitis.

Take internally to ease stress-related symptoms such as anxiety, headaches, restlessness, or nerve pain.

Drink as tea before bedtime to induce sleep or to relieve nerve pain.

CAUTION

Not appropriate for children, pregnant women, or people with high blood pressure.

Not appropriate for children, pregnant women, or people with high blood pressure.

Not for people with hypertension, glaucoma, or diabetes, or for pregnant women.

Fair-skinned individuals should avoid excessive exposure to sunlight when using this herb.

Do not drive or use dangerous equipment after taking valerian.

PREPARING HERBAL MEDICINES

The cultivation and preparation of herbal medicines is an art unto itself. Several books are listed in the References section at the back of this book that describe some of the ways to cultivate and prepare herbs. Or check the Resources section, where you can find sources for ready-made base materials to simplify your health regimen. You will find some basic guidelines below. Don't be intimidated in this section by the different methods. Preparing herbal medicines is really very simple and it is fun to experiment.

INTERNAL USES

TEA: use 1 teaspoon of dried herb or 2 teaspoons fresh herb per cup of boiling, purified water (bottled spring water). Add an extra teaspoon if brewing a pot. Steep for 10 minutes.

INFUSIONS: these are much thicker and stronger than herbal teas. The best way to prepare an infusion is to use a French press. A French press will not break with boiling water and will give you more room to extract the active qualities of the herb. You can find a French press at a specialty tea or coffee store. Start by putting 1 ounce of dried flowers or leaves of an herb into the French press. Add 3 cups of boiling, purified water (bottled spring water), cover with the lid, and let the mixture steep for 20 minutes. Strain the mixture in the press and drink in small quantities throughout the day, hot or cold. Infusions should be refrigerated and will last 3 or 4 days. They can also be used externally, added to baths, or used with compresses.

DECOCTIONS: since roots and barks require a longer extraction time, this method works best for them. Break up the bark into small pieces. Place 1 ounce of herb and 4 cups of water in an enamel or ceramic pot and allow the water to boil for about 15 minutes until it has been reduced to approximately 3 cups. Cover and steep for an additional 10 minutes. Strain and drink hot or cold, in small quantities throughout the day. Decoctions will last 3 or 4 days in the refrigerator.

TINCTURES: these liquid extracts are a convenient way to preserve the active ingredients of an herb in an alcohol or glycerin base. They are easy to make or you can save time and buy them at any health food store or check the Resources section in the back of this book. To prepare your own tinctures, combine 16 ounces of 100-proof vodka and 8 ounces of the chopped, fresh herb in a canning jar. Cap the jar tightly and allow the mixture to sit for 4 to 6 weeks. Strain and decant.

EXTERNAL USES

INFUSED OILS: fresh herbs that are infused in an oil base are an effective ally in treating a number of external conditions and are very easy to make. Using fresh herbs, discard any soiled areas of the plant. Do not wash the plant because this will encourage mold to grow. Chop up the herb and completely fill a clean, dry canning jar with the plant material. Next, add your base oil, usually quality olive or safflower oil, and fill the jar to the rim. Cover and let oil sit for 6 weeks in a cool place. Strain and decant. For a richer, more concentrated oil, double infuse the oil by packing another canning jar with fresh herbs and filling it to the rim with once-infused oil.

OINTMENTS & SALVES: these remedies are easy to make after you have already made your infused oil. Place 1 ounce of infused oil in a small pan and add 1 tablespoon of grated beeswax. Beeswax can be obtained through a craft shop or herbal apothecary. Stir over low heat until wax melts and pour into ointment jar. If the final consistency is too hard, re-melt and add more infused oil; if it is too soft, re-melt and add more beeswax.

AROMATHERAPY

Aromatherapy refers to the practice of using essential oils derived from flowers, leaves, seeds, roots, and resins of aromatic plants to promote health and well-being. The term "aromatherapy" is often misunderstood—thanks, in part, to the beauty industry. Many people think aromatherapy refers to little more than scented candles and pleasant-smelling cosmetics. In fact, aromatherapy is much more. Since antiquity, essential oils have been utilized for their healing properties. By losing touch with this heritage, we have deprived ourselves of one of the most pleasurable aspects of self-care, one that delights the senses while providing therapeutic relief to the body.

Essential oils are highly concentrated plant extracts that contain chemical compounds, mainly terpenes and phenyl propenes that work on many levels. Their chemical makeup gives essential oils many antibiotic, antiseptic, analgesic, anti-inflammatory, and antiviral properties. These characteristics, not simply their aromatic properties, make them important agents of healing. Essential oils that contain the chemical constituents called esters are relaxing and have anti-inflammatory properties while essential oils that contain phenols are stimulating and have antiseptic, bactericidal properties. This is common knowledge in Europe, where essential oils are frequently used in hospitals and other clinical settings. The French chemist Renè Maurice Gattefosse, who explored the therapeutic properties of essential oils extensively, especially their antiseptic uses, coined the term "aromatherapy." In 1910, Gattefosse discovered the therapeutic effects of lavender essential oil when a laboratory explosion left him severely burned. When he applied terpene-free lavender oil, the burns healed quickly and without any scarring.

The use of essential oils for clinical treatment is becoming a widely accepted complement to traditional allopathic medicine. Aromatherapists believe that the therapeutic effects are delivered in two ways: absorption through the skin or inhalation via the nose and bronchial passages. Essential oils may be absorbed through the skin due to their small molecular structure and because they are lipid (fat) soluble. This is similar to the action of nicotine patches.

Having penetrated the epidermis, essential oils reach the small capillaries of the dermis and enter the bloodstream to circulate throughout the body. The permeability of the skin is increased in thin-skinned areas such as the forehead and scalp as well as in areas plentiful in follicles and sweat glands. More conclusive evidence seems to indicate that when essential oils are inhaled, they enter the bloodstream very quickly through respiration. Once they enter the bloodstream, they are powerful healing agents with a wide range of applications.

Another important way that essential oils interact with our bodies is through our sense of smell. Psychoaromatherapy refers to the application of essential oils to enhance emotional well-being through either stimulating or relaxing the mind. Scents, when inhaled, stimulate the olfactory nerve endings at the bridge of the nose. This, in turn, activates the limbic system of the brain, the predominant area influencing memory, emotion, and psychological functions. This is why smell has a powerful associative effect on us: the fragrance of cedar can cause us to flash back to our grandmother's cedar closet, or the warm scent of vanilla reminds us of her kitchen. Several studies have supported the concept that certain fragrances produce mood changes, as well as enhance performance accuracy on the job. In England, a study focusing on the effects of lavender oil in relieving insomnia in a hospital setting demonstrated that it was as effective as medication and also helped improve the quality of sleep. Trials are under way in the United States to examine the calming effects of essential oils in clinical settings with Alzheimer's patients and mentally ill patients.

An important point to emphasize here is that the therapeutic properties can be achieved only through the use of genuine essential oils and not synthetic ones. Over 95% of the essential oils produced today are made for the perfume and food industries and are often adulterated. The reason for this is that genuine and pure essential oils are subject to growing conditions that can affect their yield, making it hard to count on a consistent fragrance year to year. And they are more expensive: to distill 1 pound of true rose essential oil requires 2000 pounds of rose petals! But for therapeutic value, a synthetic essential oil does not have the chemical characteristics needed to effect a change in the body.

THE ESSENTIAL OIL LIBRARY

With hundreds of essential oils on the market, the beginner can be overwhelmed trying to learn to use aromatherapy for health. The key is to begin with a few essential oils as your "backbone" and then let your creative impulses carry you from there. With practice, I have learned that just a few oils can solve myriad conditions in ways that are both pleasurable and easy.

As aromatherapy continues to grow in popularity, the number of aromatherapy companies selling high-quality, premium essential oils has, thankfully, risen as well. Most health food stores sell low-grade essential oils; if you really want to explore the world of therapeutic aromatherapy you need to contact the companies that specialize in premium essential oils. Check the Resources section in the back of this book.

Wine experts know that the pleasure felt in tasting a fine glass of wine revolves around the complicated range of tastes and textures experienced as the wine glides over your tongue. Connoisseurs commonly use words like sweet, oaky, chocolatey, buttery, pear-like and full-bodied to describe the indescribable sensation of their wines. The same holds true in the world of aromatherapy. Just as you can taste the difference between a young wine and a vintage bottle of cabernet, you can smell the difference between synthetic and genuine essential oils as well as low-grade and premium essential oils. Learn to trust your nose. Synthetic essential oils saturate the olfactory bulbs in your nasal passages quite readily. In doing so, they make it more difficult to differentiate the tonal ranges of the scent.

The term "essential oils" is somewhat of a misnomer because their texture resembles the consistency of water and not of oil. When shopping for an essential oil, try dabbing some on your fingertips. If it has a greasy base, it is not a genuine essential oil or it has been diluted in a carrier oil. Examine the price. Raw materials for essential oils are often handpicked and have to be distilled slowly at low temperatures to retain their therapeutic properties. Also, in the case of some of the finer flowers, such as roses, it takes a lot of the raw material to yield a sufficient quantity of the oil. So if the essential oils you are thinking of purchasing seem too cheap, chances are you are buying an inferior product that has been adulterated.

When purchasing essential oils it is important to select the oils by the correct Latin name. This is because there are different varieties of particular species of a plant. For example, there are several different varieties of eucalyptus; *Eucalyptus globulus, E. radiata,* and *E. citriodora* are just three. Each of these produces oil with a different scent as well as a different therapeutic action due to the chemical composition. *Eucalyptus globulus* produces the most antibacterial oil, because of its higher eucalyptol content. Different climate conditions and soil composition can also affect the chemical makeup of the essential oil.

The following essential oils are building blocks to create your home first aid kit. Refer to the chart on pages 34–37 to guide you in blending and diluting the oils for application. Carrier oils help to dilute essential oils that otherwise are too strong to apply directly to the skin (see pages 40–42).

Special precautions: In general, all the essential oils listed in this book are safe for home use. Do not take internally. During pregnancy avoid the stimulating essential oils and stick to a sedative oil such as lavender in half the stated amount.

ESSENTIAL OIL FIRST AID KIT

The following essential oils can be used to nourish the mind and body.

OIL	PROPERTIES
BAY LAUREL *(Laurus nobilis)*: Sweet, warm, spicy oil well known for its use in after-shave lotions.	antiseptic, bactericidal, antirheumatic
GERMAN CHAMOMILE *(Matricaria recutita)*: This plant looks similar to tiny daisies and has a pungent aroma of sweet apples. The essential oil is easy to identify by the bright blue color of its main ingredient, chamazulene.	anti-inflammatory, sedative
ROMAN CHAMOMILE *(Anthemis nobilis)*: Yellow essential oil with sweet scent similar to German chamomile.	antispasmodic, sedative
CLARY SAGE *(Salvia sclarea)*: The oil has a musky, nutty aroma known for its euphoric qualities.	sedative, muscle relaxant, aphrodisiac
EUCALYPTUS *(Eucalyptus globulus)*: Primarily grown and distilled in Australia, oil from the leaves of this tree is well known for its decongestant properties in treating colds.	antibacterial, antiviral, stimulates circulation
EVERLAST *(Helichrysum italicum)*: The oil yielded from the flowers of this plant is beneficial in treating skin conditions.	anti-inflammatory, antibacterial
JUNIPER *(Juniperus communis)*: Extracted from the berry, this oil has a warm camphor scent.	antiseptic, diuretic

COMMON USES

Add oil to massage blends to stimulate the lymphatic system or to promote local circulation.

Soothe dry, irritated skin conditions by mixing chamomile with a carrier oil and apply as needed. To utilize the sedative properties of chamomile, add to bath oil to reduce stress-related symptoms of insomnia, tension, or irritability.

Add to massage oils to relieve muscle spasms or ease tension.

Add to massage blends to encourage deep relaxation as a remedy for muscular tension and mental or emotional stress.

Use steam inhalation treatments to alleviate nasal congestion from colds, sinusitis, and bronchial infections. Add to massage oil to provide relief from muscular aches and pains.

Add to face oils for regenerative skin care. Speeds the healing of bruises and diminishes scars.

Use in skin care to help prevent blemishes. Add to bath oils to help kidneys flush toxins from the body.

CAUTION

Skin irritant. Always dilute in carrier oil.

Pregnant women should avoid. Use in moderation.

Use in moderation.

OIL	PROPERTIES
LAVENDER *(Lavandula angustifolia,* also called *Lavandula vera* or *Lavandula officinalis)*: Lavender is truly the most versatile of all the essential oils, making it the Swiss Army knife of aromatherapy. This deliciously fragrant oil blends well with other essential oils and has a wide variety of therapeutic uses.	antibacterial, anti-inflammatory, analgesic, sedative
MARJORAM *(Origanum majorana)*: Well known for its warm, penetrating, peppery aroma.	sedative, antispasmodic
PEPPERMINT *(Mentha piperita)*: This herb with a refreshing scent is an important ally in digestive ailments, for which it acts as a general tonic.	antispasmodic, antibacterial, stimulating
ROSEMARY *(Rosmarinus officinalis)*: A staple in most herb gardens, this plant, whose leaves have a warm, piercing aroma, is known for its stimulating effect on the mind and body.	antiseptic, analgesic, decongestant, energizing
SANDALWOOD *(Santalum album)*: A rich, resinous oil derived from rare trees that grow in the Mysore region of India.	exotic aroma is calming and grounding to the mind, aphrodisiac
TEA TREE *(Melaleuca alternifolia)*: The most versatile oil for all types of infections.	antibacterial, antiviral, antifungal
THYME *(Thymus vulgaris linalool)*: A pungent, aggressive essential oil invaluable in fighting infections.	antibacterial, antiviral

Apply compress of neat lavender oil to soothe minor burns and speed healing. Dab lavender directly on cuts or wounds to disinfect. Dilute in a carrier oil and add to bath water or massage into head, neck, and shoulders to reduce stress-related symptoms such as headaches, insomnia, anxiety, and fatigue.

Diffuse this relaxing aroma into the air to ease insomnia or combine with a base oil and add to bath to promote calm and stability. Add to massage blends to dilate blood vessels and relax cramped muscles.

Place a few drops on a tissue and inhale to relax the stomach during pregnancy or motion sickness. Diffuse peppermint oil into the air as a decongestant for colds and flu or to wake up a sluggish mind.

A potential skin irritant. Always dilute in carrier oil.

Inhale from bottle or diffuse into air to help fight mental fatigue. Add to massage blends and rub into affected areas to reduce muscular pain or rheumatism, to stimulate digestion, or to relieve headaches.

Pregnant women should avoid this stimulating essential oil.

Diffuse in atmosphere to relieve stress. Create a sensual massage oil.

Use neat on cuts, bites, acne, warts, and cold sores, to disinfect.

Add to steam inhalations to combat bronchitis or sinus infections.

Pregnant women should avoid this stimulating essential oil. Always dilute in a carrier oil to avoid skin irritation.

EXQUISITE ESSENTIAL OILS

While the Essential Oil First Aid Kit will give you a strong foundation of self-care applications for a variety of conditions, by all means treat yourself to some of the more tantalizing and exotic oils. Smell is such an individual experience. For some oils, such as rose, people either love it or hate it. There are well over a hundred different essential oils, so experiment and create your own blends. Here are some of my personal favorites that add body to blends or are wonderful to use alone.

ATLAS CEDAR *(Cedrus atlanticus)*: sweet, smoky, warm aroma; antiseptic

BASIL *(Ocimum basilicum)*: pungent, invigorating aroma; antispasmodic

BENZOIN *(Styrax benzoin)*: sweet vanilla-like scent; sedative

BERGAMOT *(Citrus bergamia)*: refreshing, green citrus; antidepressant

CARDAMOM *(Elettaria cardamomum)*: warm, spicy scent; grounding

FRANKINCENSE *(Boswellia carteri)*: smoky camphor scent; antiseptic

GRAPEFRUIT *(Citrus paradisi)*: sweet, uplifting citrus; mentally enlivening

JASMINE *(Jasminum grandiflorum)*: exotic, rich, sweet floral; aphrodisiac

LEMON *(Citrus limonum)*: invigorating citrus; bactericide

LIME *(Citrus aurantifolia)*: fresh, sharp, stimulating citrus; uplifting

NEROLI *(Citrus aurantium)*: sweet, intoxicating floral; sedative

ROSE OTTO *(Rosa damascena)*: sweet, feminine aroma; antidepressant

TANGERINE *(Citrus reticulata)*: sweet, tangy citrus; uplifting

VETIVERT *(Vetiveria zizanoides)*: rich, smoky, balsam; grounding

YLANG YLANG *(Cananga odorata)*: heady, sweet, exotic floral; euphoric

CARRIER OILS

Most essential oils besides lavender are too highly concentrated to use on the body directly because they can irritate the skin. For many recipes cited throughout this book you will find references to carrier or base oils to mix with the essential oils. Use a carrier to dilute essential oils before they are applied to the body.

Carrier oils are vegetable, nut, or seed oils, many of which have therapeutic properties themselves. All carrier oils used for aromatherapy should be cold pressed and not processed or extracted with chemical agents. The nutritive properties of carrier oils are an important part of maintaining the skin. You can use one of these carrier oils as a base for making the massage or bath oil recipes in this book, or try combining two or three of them to increase the therapeutic effect.

CARRIER OILS

SWEET ALMOND OIL: a pale yellow oil with a mild nutty aroma containing glycosides, minerals, and vitamins. Rich in protein. This medium-weight oil is the most commonly used oil for massage because it glides smoothly and lubricates the skin. Beneficial for all skin types.

APRICOT KERNEL OIL: this lightweight, pale yellow oil, rich in minerals and vitamins, is used primarily in skin care treatments because it is easily absorbed. Excellent for facial massage.

AVOCADO OIL: a dark green oil obtained from the flesh of the avocado. It is rich in fatty acids, proteins, and vitamins A, B, and C. Ideal for dry, dehydrated skin; works best if used as a 15–25% dilution with another, lighter oil such as apricot kernel oil.

BORAGE SEED OIL: a pale yellow oil, rich in gamma linolenic acid (GLA), an essential fatty acid that assists in cellular regeneration. Borage seed oil has skin rejuvenating properties and is excellent for stretch marks or prematurely aged skin. Works best if used in a 10% dilution with another oil such as sweet almond or grapeseed.

CALOPHYLLUM INOPHYLLUM OIL: this green oil with a nutty maple scent is extracted from the fruit and seeds of a large tree that is indigenous to Madagascar. It is beneficial for acute skin irritations and to strengthen connective tissues. Use in a 10% dilution with another carrier oil.

COCONUT OIL: natural coconut oil solidifies at room temperature but fractionated coconut oil remains fluid and is a medium-weight carrier oil for massage. It is used commonly in Indonesia for its emollient properties.

EVENING PRIMROSE OIL: this pale yellow oil has the highest gamma linolenic content of any carrier oil and is invaluable in treating dry skin conditions or in preventing scar tissue. Use in a 10% dilution with a lightweight oil such as apricot kernel.

GRAPESEED OIL: this pale green oil is exceptionally light. It can be used on its own or makes a nice blend with other, heavier-weight massage oils.

HAZELNUT OIL: this pale yellow oil has a strong nutty aroma and a slight astringent action making it ideal in skin care for individuals with slightly oily complexions. Use in a 10% dilution with another light carrier oil such as apricot kernel.

JOJOBA OIL: this yellow oil is actually a wax derived from a bean. The chemical structure of jojoba resembles sebum and therefore is recommended in skin care for acne-prone individuals because it will not clog pores.

OLIVE OIL: this green oil is rich in chlorophyll, proteins, minerals, and vitamins. It is often used in conjunction with lighter-textured oils to make a less viscous oil.

ROSE HIP SEED OIL: this pale yellow, lightweight oil is rich in vitamins and contains up to 50% gamma linolenic acid. It is a popular carrier oil for tissue regeneration, especially to treat scarring and wound healing, or for mature skin. Use in a 10% dilution with another carrier oil.

SAFFLOWER OIL: this pale yellow oil has a medium-weight texture and is useful as a massage oil alone or blended with other carrier oils.

SUNFLOWER OIL: this golden colored oil has a slight nutty aroma and serves as a multipurpose massage oil or can be combined with other carrier oils.

WHEAT GERM OIL: this slightly orange oil is full of vitamins, especially vitamin E, making it a powerful antioxidant. It stimulates skin regeneration and, due to high antioxidant properties, it is useful to add up to 15% in massage blends to prevent rancidity.

By adding herbs to carrier oils, therapeutic properties are enhanced. Flowers or leaves of the herb are gently bruised or chopped to release their active properties and added to the carrier oil. This is called an herbal infused oil. Below are some herbal infused oils that can benefit your blends; instructions for making herbal infused oils are on pages 29 and 117–118.

HERBAL INFUSED OILS

ARNICA OIL: this infused oil is effective in the treatment of bruises, aches, strains, and swellings. It is also useful in the treatment of joint pain. Use in a 10% dilution with another carrier oil.

CALENDULA OIL: also known as pot marigold, calendula is prized for its anti-inflammatory properties. As an infused oil, it is excellent for dry skin, minor burns, and irritated skin conditions. Use in a 10% dilution with another carrier oil.

CHAMOMILE OIL: Roman chamomile *(Anthemis nobilis)* is valuable for its anti-spasmodic and sedative properties and can be used in massage for muscular pain and to ease nervous tension. Use in a 10% dilution with another carrier oil.

ST. JOHN'S WORT OIL: used externally, this herb is excellent for wound healing and aggravated skin conditions. This infused oil has a rich, ruby red color and is very effective in treating psoriasis, eczema, dermatitis, and minor burns. Use in a 10% dilution with another carrier oil.

Alchemy is a word I have always loved, and the blending of essential oils is the perfect way to get back in touch with our inner mad scientist. As a general rule, since essential oils are quite strong and can irritate the skin, when applying them to the body it is always best to dilute them in a base or carrier oil, usually a nut or vegetable oil such as almond, grapeseed, or safflower oil. (See carrier oils, pages 40–42.) Essential oils are light-sensitive, so be sure to store in dark glass bottles away from direct light sources. Always use glass bottles to blend and store essential oils since the oils can be very aggressive and will corrode certain materials such as some types of plastic.

One beauty of working with essential oils is that since they are so potent you do not need to use much to achieve a desired effect. Essential oils are 75 to 100 times more concentrated than dried herbs, making them an extremely powerful and efficient method of healing. For an effective treatment you will want to blend the oils at a 2 or 3% dilution ratio; in other words, for a 4-ounce bottle of carrier oil, add 48 drops of essential oil (2 oz. = 24 drops, 1oz. = 12 drops). This is a classic case of less is more—try to resist the temptation to put too much of an essential oil in a blend to get a strong aroma. With genuine essential oils you need less to get a therapeutic effect. Be wary of the preblended oils you may find at stores that bombard your nose the minute you open the cap.

USING ESSENTIAL OILS

Use the following chart as your reference guide in using essential oils.

METHOD	DILUTION
MASSAGE OIL	Take a 1-ounce bottle and fill halfway with a carrier oil such as almond, apricot kernel, or grapeseed oil. Add 12 drops of an essential oil, shake well, and top off with carrier oil.
BATH OIL	Dilute the same way as massage oil.
INHALATION	Make a steam tent by using your bathroom sink. Close drain and fill clean sink with hot water. Add 4–5 drops of essential oils to steaming water, place a large towel over your head and shoulders, breathe deeply through your nose.
COMPRESS	Add 2–3 drops to water.
SAUNA	Add 3–4 drops to 1 quart of water and gradually throw cupfuls onto heat source.
SHOWER	Use plastic $1/2$-ounce bottle with a flip lid to prevent spilling. Fill halfway with carrier oil, add 6 drops of essential oil, shake well, and top off with carrier oil.
VAPORIZATION	Add 4–5 drops of essential oil to aroma lamp, lightbulb ring, electric or candle diffuser, or humidifier.

SUGGESTIONS

Use an amber or blue glass bottle (available at health food stores or see the Resources section in the back of the book).

Add bath oil to still water so that the volatile essential oils do not evaporate.

Heat a tea kettle on stove and add a little at a time to sink for extra steam. For traveling, apply 2–3 drops to handkerchief or tissue and sniff when needed.

Fill clean sink or bowl with warm or cool water. Add essential oils and swish water to disperse. Soak washcloth in water, wring out, and apply to face or other affected area.

Never add essential oils directly to heat source—they are flammable.

Apply 1 teaspoon of blend to damp washcloth or sponge and rub vigorously onto body under running water. Keep away from eyes.

Diffusers, whether candlelit or electric, are a great way to scent a room. As the lamp heats up, oils are released into the air.

3 SPRING

SPRING

Spring is a time of renewal, transition, and unevenness.

In snowy climates, the ground thaws long enough for us to see the crocuses and daffodils bloom and then freezes again. Forced to stay indoors, we grow restless.

This is a perfect time to nurture ourselves inwardly, to realign our mind and body to our natural rhythms. To do this we have to consciously unplug from the fast-paced environment that surrounds us.

One way to find a natural rhythm is to have a time moratorium. Make a conscious decision that when you come home from work you will take your watch off and, along with it, the mantle of work-related responsibilities. Better still, try spending an entire day on a weekend without using any type of timepiece or electrical appliance such as a television or radio. Cover the clocks in your home or place them in a drawer and do not wear a watch. Begin the day by waking up when your body tells you to rise and not at some predetermined hour. Make your meals when your stomach starts rumbling and not when your watch tells you to. You will be surprised at how incredibly long the day will seem as you consciously celebrate idleness without the ticking of the clock. Spread out on the sofa and take a nap. Pull a comfortable chair up to the window and watch the sun crawl across the sky. Spend some time sitting quietly and focusing on your breath. As you become relaxed, observe what thoughts come up and be present with those feelings instead of rushing onward to the next activity. Giving yourself this reflective time is a good elixir for an overstimulated mind.

Spring is also a time to create rituals of rejuvenation to combat stress and fatigue and to lift us up from feeling depressed by the still short days. Psycho-aromatherapy is very effective in this regard by creating an uplifting, warm ambiance. Purchase a ceramic electric or candle diffuser and try the uplifting citrus oils such as grapefruit, orange, lime, or mandarin. Cardamom or the woodland oils such as pine, cedar, or juniper are also effective. You can diffuse one essential oil at a time or try some of the synergistic blends outlined in this section to vaporize in your home.

Traditional natural healers such as herbalists and naturopathic doctors advise taking time in the spring to create detoxification rituals. The idea that the body needs to detoxify can be overexaggerated, as the body naturally is very effective in cleansing itself. Many people become fixated on the concept of purging the body of parasites, yeasts, and toxins, with the idea that the body can reach a state of purity. This is a very punishing concept and one that has consumed human consciousness from early times, prompting ancient practices such as bloodletting. A far healthier notion is to support the body's own ability to detoxify via the circulatory and lymphatic system. In this section, you will find recipes to help bolster this approach.

Is there really such a thing as spring fever? Absolutely—true spring fever occurs when a cool spell is followed by sudden warmth and our body is slow to catch up. The quick changes in temperatures during the spring months often make us susceptible to illness, especially colds and flu. Ginger, because of its stimulating and warming qualities, is often used in Chinese medicine to treat conditions related to cold and dampness. One of the best cold and flu treatments is to stimulate a natural immune response by sweating out the cold. This cold remedy, with the diaphoretic action of the ginger and cinnamon, is not only effective at the first sign of a chill or cold. It is also a powerful immune system stimulant because of the ability of Siberian ginseng to build resistance to disease. Ginseng also improves vitality and stamina. Best of all, this drink tastes heavenly.

Makes 1 quart

2 ripe Anjou pears, peeled, seeded, and cored

3 cups apple juice concentrate, unsweetened (100% juice)

3 teaspoons fresh grated ginger

1/4 teaspoon cinnamon

1/8 teaspoon nutmeg

20 drops Siberian ginseng (*Eleutherococcus senticosus*) tincture

Cut pears into quarters and combine with apple juice, ginger, cinnamon, and nutmeg in blender. Blend until smooth; chill. Pour into glass, add 20 drops of Siberian ginseng tincture, and stir. Drink 3 times daily.

Special precautions: This type of ginseng works slowly. Take for 3 weeks, rest for 1 week, then repeat cycle. Ginseng is not an appropriate remedy for children or pregnant women. If you are taking over-the-counter prescriptions or have high blood pressure, you should consult a physician before taking ginseng.

MANDARIN LIME SYNERGY

One of the reasons aromatherapy has become so popular is that it enables us to alter our moods and our energy levels through the use of fragrant, natural scent. Refreshing your home with essential oils is like being able to throw a new coat of paint onto your walls and create a new ambiance.

A synergy of essential oils is a combination of two or more oils blended together to heighten the therapeutic effect. Synergies are more powerful than the individual essential oils. The warm notes of basil and marjoram are revitalizing. The uplifting qualities of citrus oils are a perfect antidepressant for the darker months before full spring.

Using a candle diffuser, simply fill the dish at the top of the diffuser with the following synergy, light the candle, and enjoy the uplifting aroma as it vaporizes into the room.

Makes 4 ounces

4-ounce glass bottle

4 ounces purified water

2 drops basil *(Ocymum basilicum)* essential oil

19 drops mandarin *(Citrus reticulata)* essential oil

21 drops lime *(Citrus aurantifolia)* essential oil

12 drops sandalwood *(Santalum album)* essential oil

12 drops grapefruit *(Citrus paradisi)* essential oil

Fill the bottle halfway with water. Add essential oils, cover, and shake well. Top off bottle with water, cover, and agitate a second time. To dispense, pour 2 tablespoons of synergy into top of diffuser. Shake well before dispensing.

In cold climates, waiting for the first bloom of spring can be agonizing. Outdoors, the landscape appears lifeless and monochromatic against the sky. Evergreen trees, with their deep, rich color, provide some contrast for our weary eyes, and the sweet, balsamic scent of their needles is reviving. This synergistic blend brings some of that warm, woody fragrance into your home. The smoky, sweet notes of atlas cedar combined with the peppery, balsamic notes of the juniper are cleansing and restorative. The fresh, green scent of bergamot balances the blend.

Makes 4 ounces

4-ounce glass bottle

4 ounces purified water

21 drops atlas cedar *(Cedrus atlanticus)* essential oil

15 drops juniper *(Juniperus communis)* essential oil

8 drops bergamot *(Citrus bergamia)* essential oil

Fill the bottle halfway with water. Add essential oils, cover, and shake well. Top off bottle with water, cover, and agitate a second time. To dispense, pour 2 tablespoons of synergy into top of diffuser. Shake well before dispensing.

HERBAL SKIN SOOTHER

This rich, nutritive body oil, fortified with soothing herbs and essential oils, will calm even the most aggravated skin conditions. When we alternately expose our skin to cold spring air followed by the warm dry air of central heating systems, the skin often becomes dry and itchy. St. John's wort is an excellent herb for this condition. Lately, St. John's wort is getting a lot of attention as an antidepressant, but this is not a recipe for depressed skin! Few people know that this is one of the best herbs to use externally for dermatitis, psoriasis, eczema, and minor burns. Rich, vanilla-like benzoin and earthy German chamomile work synergistically for their anti-inflammatory properties while rose and sandalwood are antiseptic to the skin.

Makes 4 ounces

4-ounce glass bottle

1/2 ounce St. John's wort infused oil
(see pages 43, 117–118)

1 ounce avocado oil

2 drops rose otto *(Rosa damascena)* **essential oil**

4 drops sandalwood *(Santalum album)* essential oil

5 drops German chamomile **(*Matricaria recutita)* essential oil**

18 drops benzoin *(Styrax benzoin)* **essential oil**

2 1/2 ounces grapeseed oil

Fill the bottle partway with 1/2 ounce of St. John's wort oil and 1 ounce avocado oil as the carrier. Add essential oils and shake well. Top off with grapeseed oil and agitate again. Apply to body as needed after bath or shower.

This herbal beverage heralds the rejuvenating properties of spring. Burdock is known as an excellent blood purifier. Burdock root is a nourishing tonic providing optimum support for the liver and kidneys as well as the circulatory and lymphatic system. It is rich in iron and other minerals and is an excellent source of vitamin C. Burdock root has an excellent reputation as a skin tonic, for symptoms including blemishes, dermatitis, psoriasis, or eczema. Burdock works slowly on the system, so take it over a period of at least three months. Licorice root works in conjunction with burdock as a blood purifier and adds sweetness to the tonic. The stimulating properties of cardamom, clove, and cinnamon bring warmth to the blend and the orange peel adds an extra dose of vitamin C.

Makes 1 quart

1/4 **cup dried, cut burdock root**
   (Arctium lappa)
1/4 **cup dried, cut licorice root**
   (Glycyrrhiza glabra)
1 **teaspoon cardamom seeds**
   (Elettaria cardamomum), crushed
3 **whole cloves**
1/4 **teaspoon cinnamon powder**
1 **tablespoon dried orange peel**
Purified water

Place all ingredients in a French press. Fill the press to the top with purified boiling water, cover and let steep for 20 minutes. Strain the tonic and drink warm or chilled, 1/2 –1 cup a day. Store in refrigerator to keep fresh.

Special precautions: Licorice root in large doses can increase blood pressure and may not be appropriate for individuals with hypertension, diabetes, glaucoma, or heart disease. Pregnant women should avoid licorice and burdock root.

Time-saver tip: You can get the benefits of burdock root in tincture form by adding 15–30 drops of extract into juice or tea and taking 3 times a day for a 3-month period.

LAVENDER COMPRESS

This is a great way to wake up on those crisp spring mornings when getting out of bed can be difficult. The restorative, anti-inflammatory properties of lavender help soothe puffy eyes and calm irritated skin, while the floral herbaceous scent helps wake up your tired mind. In addition, the warm, steaming washcloth helps the essential oil penetrate the skin more easily.

Fill clean bathroom sink with warm water. Add 2–3 drops of lavender *(Lavandula vera)* essential oil and swish water to disperse the oil. Soak washcloth in water, wring out, and apply to face. Inhale deeply.

NEROLI COMPLEXION SERUM

This fragrant face oil will nourish and tone the skin. Exposure to the elements and over-heated homes during cooler months are two reasons people experience dry skin. Other culprits are synthetic soaps and alcohol-based toners, which strip moisture from the skin. People often assume that their faces are clean when the skin feels tight after cleansing, but this is really just the surfactants removing the good oils that protect your skin. Most people are reluctant to apply oils to their face for fear that it will clog the pores or cause the skin to break out. This is absolutely not true if you are using genuine essential oils and an organic carrier oil. In Europe, oils for the face are an accepted part of skin care. This complexion serum has a base of hazelnut oil, which is slightly astringent and is absorbed quite readily into the skin, and borage seed oil, which is high in gamma linoleic acid, a fatty acid found in collagen. These oils alone will feed the skin better than any synthetic compounds found in commercial cosmetic preparations. Neroli is particularly valuable in this blend for its ability to regulate activity of the capillaries and restore vitality to the skin.

Makes ½ ounce

½-ounce glass bottle

¼ ounce hazelnut oil

1 drop lavender *(Lavandula vera)* **essential oil**

2 drops sandalwood *(Santalum album)* **essential oil**

2 drops rose *(Rosa damascena)* **essential oil**

3 drops neroli *(Citrus aurantium)* **essential oil**

¼ ounce borage seed oil

Fill the bottle partway with hazelnut oil. Add essential oils, cover, and shake well. Top off with borage seed oil, cover, and agitate a second time. To use, apply 3–4 drops to moist cotton pad and wipe over damp face. For added benefit, use in conjunction with floral waters (see page 120) and burdock root tincture (see page 57).

Dragon well tea, also known as Lung Ching, is the best known and prized of Chinese green teas. It is grown in the Tieh Mu mountains of the Zhejiang Province and has a sweet, mossy flavor. As opposed to black teas, green teas are not fermented and have much less caffeine. The withered leaves of the *Camellia sinesis* plant are steamed to prevent enzymes from reacting to oxygen and causing fermentation. Green tea is ingested several times a day in Japan as a tonic, and it has a widespread reputation as a valuable antioxidant to fight cancer and other diseases. Scientists believe it helps prevent heart disease because the catechins, a lipid-lowering ingredient in green tea, assist in lowering cholesterol.

Drinking green tea several times a day is an excellent substitute for coffee. Coffee increases anxiety and irritability and, because of its high acid content, often causes digestive upsets. Also, the heavy oils in coffee beans exacerbate a sluggish liver. Try cutting down on your coffee intake and substituting green tea instead.

1 teaspoon dragon well tea leaves

1 cup purified water

Bring water to a gentle boil and pour over tea leaves. Steep for 30 seconds to 3 minutes. Strain.

Special precautions: Green tea is naturally more astringent than black tea and care should be taken that the tea does not steep too long or it will become bitter.

HEALING CALENDULA SALVE

My mother was an avid gardener all her life and cracked skin on her hands was a testament to her passion for working the soil. (She always swore that Bag Balm, a salve originally created to soothe cow's udders and loaded with mineral oil, did the trick.)

This all-natural salve contains my favorite herb for treating dry skin. It has a base of soothing beeswax, which acts as an emollient barrier to protect the skin. Beeswax is easy to find at a health food store or check the Resources section in the back of the book. The anti-inflammatory properties of calendula make it a versatile remedy for healing wounds, scratches, or minor burns. This salve is invaluable in the cooler months for dry elbows or cracked skin. Calendula has a delicious honeylike bouquet, which makes the salve all the more irresistible!

Makes ½ ounce

Heatproof glass measuring cup
½ ounce calendula infused oil (see page 118)
½ tablespoon beeswax, grated
5 drops benzoin extract
4 drops lavender *(Lavandula vera)* essential oil
½-ounce glass ointment jar

Pour calendula infused oil and beeswax into the heatproof glass measuring cup. Place cup in a shallow pan of simmering water. Heat, stirring constantly, until all the ingredients are melted together. Add benzoin extract and lavender essential oil and stir until well mixed. Pour into ointment jar and place in refrigerator to set. Apply liberally to body as needed.

Massage, one of the oldest healing arts, is a powerful antidote to stress. For some people, massage therapy still sounds like a luxury, an indulgent form of pampering rather than a health benefit, but it has many physiological benefits. It improves circulation of blood and movement of lymph fluids, reduces blood pressure, strengthens the immune system, relieves muscle tension and stiffness, and aids in relaxation of the entire body. During a massage we become aware of where we unconsciously hold stress in our bodies and are then better able to let go of that tension.

Equally important are the mental health benefits of massage. Studies at the University of Miami School of Medicine's Touch Research Institute demonstrated that premature infants who were massaged developed more quickly and were less irritable. Touch is equally important to adults because everyone has a need to be cared for, and nurturing touch fosters a sense of well-being. Similar to meditation, massage anchors us and enhances calm thinking and clarity.

While it may be more relaxing to receive a massage from a professional massage therapist or a partner, you can still experience the benefits of touch through self-massage. Self-massage feels great and helps relieve tension in forgotten areas.

Lower Body: Sit with legs crossed and begin with the feet. Grab one foot with both hands, and using a wringing motion, gently wring the foot between your hands. Using small, circular thumb movements, trace five parallel lines on the bottom of your foot by pressing into the sole of the foot at the heel and continuing up to the toes. This movement is the basis for reflexology, a specialized form of massage based on the theory that the soles of the feet reflect other organs or areas of the body. Continue massaging up the body by gently squeezing the calf muscle to relieve tension.

Middle Body: Using small, circular movements with the fingers of both hands, massage the lower back beginning at the base of the spine on the sacrum. Work laterally out to the hips. Next, massage the abdomen in a clockwise direction to help stimulate the digestive movement of the colon. This is helpful for relieving constipation or gas.

Upper Body: To release tension stored in the chest and upper body, use small, circular movements with your fingers to relax the pectoral muscles, working from the breastbone out to the arms. To relieve headaches and eye strain, circle the temples with the middle fingers and continue the circular movements around the ear and underneath the base of the skull.

Rub the scalp vigorously with the pads of your fingers to stimulate circulation and ease tension. To release shoulder tightness, grab the trapezius muscle between your thumb and four fingers and squeeze gently.

Stress Relief Massage Oils

Stress can affect us in a variety of ways. Sometimes the body becomes overstimulated, such as when we are trying to meet an important deadline. We become agitated, nervous, or anxious. A remedy in this situation is to use essential oils that will relax the central nervous system and ground us. At other times when stress becomes overwhelming, we may turn inward and become lethargic or depressed. Preparing a blend that will stimulate or energize us is the key here and can be used to treat conditions like jet lag. Use for full-body massage or apply to specific areas such as the soles of the feet or chest area to reduce tension.

The smoky, musky notes of sandalwood and vetivert in this blend are very grounding to the mind while the soft floral notes of jasmine add a hint of sweetness to the oil. This is a powerful antidote to relax overstimulated nervous systems. Use this massage oil before going to bed.

Makes 1 ounce

1-ounce glass bottle

1 ounce carrier oil (select one or a combination of several carrier oils on pages 40–42)

5 drops sandalwood *(Santalum album)* **essential oil**

4 drops vetivert *(Vetiveria zizanoides)* **essential oil**

3 drops jasmine *(Jasminum grandi florum)* **essential oil**

Fill the bottle halfway with carrier oil. Add essential oils and shake well. Top off with remaining carrier oil, cover, and agitate a second time. Apply where needed.

Energizing Cardamom Balsam

This energizing blend is a good remedy for jet lag or for periods of intense stress such as exam time. The stimulating, refreshing quality of grapefruit and cardamom help combat exhaustion while the soothing properties of lavender act as a tonic for the nervous system. The woody balsamic tone of the cedar helps to restore equilibrium to the body.

Makes 1 ounce

1-ounce glass bottle

1 ounce carrier oil (select one or a combination of several carrier oils on pages 40–42)

3 drops atlas cedar (*Cedrus atlanti cus*) essential oil

5 drops grapefruit (*Citrus paradisi*) essential oil

3 drops lavender (*Lavandula vera*) essential oil

2 drops cardamom (*Ellettaria cardamomum*) essential oil

Fill the bottle halfway with carrier oil. Add essential oils and shake well. Top off with remaining carrier oil, cover, and agitate a second time. Apply where needed.

Long hours on the phone or in front of a computer often produce stress headaches. The sharp, piercing pain that is characteristic of these episodes usually has its source in the tight trapezius muscles of the upper neck and shoulder. Getting up often from your desk and stretching for several minutes is the best preventive measure.

This aromatherapy blend will help ease the pain once a headache is under way and is a useful remedy to keep in your desk drawer. Lavender calms the central nervous system and helps ease tension while the camphorous notes of the peppermint act as a stimulant as well as an antispasmodic. The combination of sedative and stimulant is a property found in many commercial pain-relieving preparations. If headache is severe, pour 1 teaspoon of the blend onto a cold compress such as a damp washcloth and apply to forehead and temples.

Makes 1 ounce

1-ounce glass bottle with dropper

1 ounce carrier oil (select one or a combination of several carrier oils on pages 40–42)

4 drops lavender (*Lavandula vera*) **essential oil**

8 drops peppermint (*Mentha piperata*) **essential oil**

Fill the bottle halfway with carrier oil. Add essential oils and shake well. Top off with remaining carrier oil, cover, and agitate a second time. Apply where needed. Squeeze one dropper of blend into palm of hand and massage temples, forehead, and back of skull.

DEEP SLEEP TEA

This delicious tea will help take the edge off of a stressful day while you enjoy these fragrant, aromatic herbs. Insomnia, while being a symptom of stress, can be triggered by many factors. Sleep disturbances caused by emotional factors such as grief or depression are best treated with essential oils that have a calming effect on the mind. When sleep disorders are caused by overstimulation due to long hours at work or jet lag, a powerful sedative herb will usually do the trick. This tea is a combination of three gentle, calming herbs that help ease nervous tension: lemon balm, chamomile, and linden blossom. Valerian tincture, a powerful sedative, can be added to the tea to enhance the effect. This herb has long been recognized for its tranquilizing effect and was quite popular in the nineteenth century for treating nervous disorders. (It is not, however, in any way similar to Valium, a prescription sedative.)

Makes 1 cup

1 cup purified water
½ teaspoon dried lemon balm leaves
½ teaspoon dried chamomile flowers
½ teaspoon dried linden blossom
    flowers
15 to 30 drops valerian tincture
    (optional)

Bring water to a boil and pour over herbs. Steep for 5 minutes. Strain and serve immediately. For increased effect, add 15–30 drops of valerian tincture to tea.

Special precautions: Valerian is quite strong so be sure not to drive while taking it. It has a strong scent that many people find disagreeable; add a slice of lemon and a teaspoon of honey if you find valerian unpleasant.

The lymphatic system, in conjunction with the circulatory system, is an important mechanism for eliminating toxins from the body. The lymphatic system is part of the body's immune system and consists of a network of fluid-filled vessels distributed throughout the body just under the surface of the skin. This system contributes to the body's defenses in two ways: by collecting bacteria and toxins from the tissues and disposing of them and by producing lymphocytes that act as antibodies for the immune system. Occasionally, impaired lymphatic flow results in the buildup of waste materials in the tissues and in the lymph nodes. The lymphatic system can benefit from being stimulated manually.

Body brushing is an old European self-care technique that takes only a few minutes to do before you step into the bath or shower. It helps remove the buildup of dead skin cells and helps stimulate the lymphatic system to eliminate toxins. The light, brisk strokes provide the right pressure on the surface of the skin and, when applied in the direction of the lymphatic routes, assist the flow of the lymph through the channels.

Body Brushing

Purchase a soft vegetable bristle brush, available at most health food stores, and rub a drop of a mild essential oil like lavender *(Lavandula vera)* on the brush to sterilize it. Using a light, sweeping stroke, begin at the feet and work up the legs front and back toward the torso. Always stroke toward the center of the body to encourage lymph flow toward the main lymphatic ducts underneath the collarbones. Brush up both sides of the arms and across the shoulders, and continue up the back and neck. Finish the treatment with small circular strokes on the abdomen in a clockwise direction following the movement of the colon.

BAY LAUREL DETOX BLEND

Follow body brushing with a massage to improve the flow of circulation. This blend encourages the removal of waste materials. Bay laurel is a potent antibacterial essential oil, while basil and rosemary stimulate local circulation in the tissues to help diminish fluid retention or sluggish circulation. This massage oil is excellent for premenstrual women who experience breast tenderness, or immune-compromised individuals who want to stimulate the lymphatic system.

Makes 1 ounce

1-ounce glass bottle

1 ounce carrier oil (select one or a combination of several carrier oils on pages 40–42)

3 drops basil *(Ocymum basilicum)* **essential oil**

4 drops rosemary *(Rosmarinus officinalis)* **essential oil**

6 drops bay laurel *(Laurus nobilis)* **essential oil**

Fill the bottle halfway with carrier oil. Add essential oils, cover, and shake well. Fill with remaining carrier oil. Cover and agitate a second time. Massage gently into lymph nodes in neck area, underneath arms, and above groin, or use for full-body massage.

One good way to cleanse the body is to give up a vice for a period of time. Whether it is sweets, soft drinks, alcohol, or whatever your particular craving is, not only allows the body to rest but lets you know who is in control, you or your demons.

Periodic short fasts—one day per month—are an effective way to cleanse your system. By not eating, you rest the digestive system and allow the body to use that energy for healing. Short-term fasting affects our emotional and mental health as well. Fasting leaves us feeling energized, clearer, and more centered. Be sure to fast on a day when you can conserve your energy. Drink lots of water and always break your fast gently with light, plain foods.

CLEANSING TONIC

Since bitter herbs help to stimulate sluggish digestion, this tonic contains lime juice to help tone the digestive system along with maple syrup, which counteracts the sour taste of the blend. Cayenne helps to stimulate digestive secretions essential to good digestion.

Makes 1/2 gallon

1/2 gallon (64 ounces) purified water

1 cup maple syrup

1 cup lime juice

1 teaspoon cayenne

Place the water, maple syrup, lime juice, and cayenne in a container. Cover and shake well. Drink one 8-ounce glass of cleansing tonic fol-lowed by one 8-ounce glass of water, 6–8 times a day.

Special precautions: Since cayenne increases digestive secretions do not ingest cayenne if you suffer from gastrointestinal problems such as ulcers or are prone to acid stomach. Discontinue fast if you feel dizzy, lightheaded, or nauseated.

DANDELION TONIC

This delicious drink will nourish your body with vitamins and minerals. The roots of the dandelion are one of the best remedies for aiding and supporting the liver. Dandelion root is high in iron, protein, and carotenes, especially vitamin A. The liver, along with the kidneys, is responsible for filtering the blood and removing toxins. Signs of a sluggish liver are dark circles under the eyes, headaches, and lack of energy, usually due to rich foods, alcohol, and stress. Drink this tonic if your diet has become one of overindulgence. Parsley, an effective diuretic, will also help flush excess fluids out of the system.

Makes 1 cup

1 cup tomato or V-8 juice (low
   sodium)
1/2 teaspoon lemon juice
1/2 teaspoon lime juice
1 tablespoon chopped fresh parsley
1 teaspoon Worcestershire sauce
Pinch of cayenne pepper
15–30 drops of dandelion root
   (*Taraxacum officinalis*) tincture

Combine all the ingredients in a blender and blend until smooth.

SUMMER

As the daylight hours grow longer, the sun's warmth relaxes our bodies and the sweet liberation of summer finally arrives.

Released from the need for layers of clothing, we can move unrestricted, free to explore the elements. Lying under the stars, swimming in the lake or ocean, or strolling barefoot releases us from the confinement of the darker months. We run outdoors thirsty to stimulate our senses and the natural world seduces us.

During the summer, time evaporates in our attempts to fit all of our plans into each day. Time flies with early morning walks, gardening, and beach picnics at dusk. Before we know it summer's end is on the horizon. Ironically, having fun becomes stressful with vacation plans and visiting friends. The challenge of summer is to slow down the momentum, to fully experience the richness of the season. Now is the time to take your meditation practice outdoors and let the sound of the ocean waves and the warmth of the sun calm your mind. As each new thought pops into your consciousness, let it float past you and not take it with you. Immerse yourself in the feeling of focused awareness.

The simple rituals of summer allow us to pause and savor the moment using all the lush resources that nature provides us. The abundance of flowers is a feast for the eyes and the air is thick with fragrance. We can replenish our bodies with fresh flowers or herbs from the garden or kitchen windowsill. Planting an herbal garden is easy to do, requires little maintenance, and can provide an abundance of fresh natural remedies to heal yourself during the summer or throughout the year.

Now is the time to use the fresh herbs and flowers of summer to boost your vitality and fortify your body. In the following pages you will find recipes for rejuvenating tonics and teas to rebuild your strength. Of course, being outdoors can create problems with insect bites and excess sun exposure—you will find first aid solutions in the following recipes as well.

This chapter invites you to explore the sensual pleasure of summer. This time of year is an aromatic cornucopia of freshly mowed grass mingled with honeysuckle, lavender, and wild rose. Indulge yourself in the fragrant bouquets of flowers and herbs from the garden to refresh your body.

The ideal way to receive the therapeutic benefits of herbs and flowers is directly from the garden. The fragrant scent of rambling honeysuckle or potted geraniums or the sweet smell of the earth following a late afternoon thundershower is euphoric. The simple ritual of cultivating and harvesting your own herbs is a meditative endeavor that is deeply satisfying.

Some herbs take no effort whatsoever to cultivate and can be found growing wild in your yard or an adjacent field. Dandelion, red clover, and burdock are all examples of common herbs that can be easily wildcrafted, if you can be sure of gathering from an unsprayed, uncontaminated area. Other therapeutic plants such as those listed on pages 24–27 you will need to plant yourself. These herbs can be ordered or purchased at your local nursery. Arnica, calendula, chamomile, echinacea, Saint John's wort, skullcap, and valerian are all important staples to your herbal remedy chest and will be invaluable healing agents throughout the year. You will want to add to this list common culinary herbs that also have therapeutic effects such as basil, lemon balm, marjoram, rosemary, oregano, peppermint, thyme, and verbena. There are some wonderful, unusual herbal hybrids now and you may want to experiment with such varieties as lemon basil, orange mint, or pineapple mint. Most of these herbs are hardy perennials that will return to your garden every spring.

Don't forget the aromatherapeutic benefits of your garden: fragrant flowers such as lavender, rose geranium, marigold, and rose are perfect as fresh cuttings to adorn a table and to make an infusion of leaves and petals for herbal teas.

Harvesting Herbs

Ideally herbs should be harvested when they are at the peak of maturity just before flowering. This is when an herb possesses the most active chemical constituents. Pick the herbs when there is absolutely no dew or other moisture on them and tie them into a small bundle with string. Hang the herbs upside down in a warm, dark, well-ventilated room. A garden shed or storage shed is perfect. Take down the herbs when the leaves are brittle, usually in about seven days. Remove the stem and store the leaves in a dark, airtight container. Dried leaves and flowers should last approximately six months if stored in suitable conditions.

Medicinal Window Box

Urban residents who do not have the luxury of garden space to grow their herbs can still prepare an herbal remedy chest with a well-designed window box. Many culinary herbs will thrive in a sunny window box and can be easily harvested to make a variety of home remedies. Listed below are some good staples for a medicinal window box.

LEMON BALM:
this delicious herb yields a pleasant-tasting, relaxing tea.

PEPPERMINT:
these leaves make a good digestive tea for upset stomach.

ROSEMARY:
this is a strong stimulating herb useful for massage oils.

GERMAN CHAMOMILE:
this calming herb can be sipped at bedtime to ease insomnia.

THYME:
this is one of the strongest antiseptic herbs, useful in inhalations for bronchial infections.

During the warmer summer months, it is refreshing to bring the delicate floral scents inside your home. These mood-enhancing fragrances have multifaceted scents whose effect upon your olfactory receptors is like a stroll in the garden. This blend combines the sweet exotic notes of ylang ylang, native to tropical Asia, with the rich floral jasmine for an intoxicating and powerfully sedative effect. Both of these essences are revered for their strong aphrodisiac properties, which seems an appropriate effect for the summer months! Musky sandalwood adds a warm, grounding note to the blend.

Makes 4 ounces

4-ounce glass bottle

4 ounces purified water

18 drops ylang ylang *(Cananga odorata)* **essential oil**

7 drops jasmine *(Jasminum grandiflorum)* **essential oil**

16 drops sandalwood *(Santalum album)* **essential oil**

Fill the bottle halfway with water. Add essential oils, cover, and shake well. Top off bottle with water, cover, and agitate a second time. To dispense, pour 2 tablespoons of synergy into top of diffuser. Shake well before dispensing.

Rose Geranium Tea

This delicious herbal tea is brimming with two of my favorite summer florals: geranium and rose. In addition to the aromatic beauty of this fragrant tea, both florals are traditionally known for their therapeutic effect in relieving nervous tension and easing depression. This calming effect is further enhanced by lemon balm, a gentle herb with a mintlike flavor. Red clover is fortified with vitamin E and has a reputation as a blood cleanser and immune enhancer.

Makes 2 cups

12 fresh red clover blossoms

2 ounces fresh lemon balm
   leaves, bruised

8 fresh peppermint leaves, bruised

3 rose geranium leaves, bruised

Petals of one rose

2 cups purified water

Combine all the herbal ingredients in a French press. Pour in the freshly boiled purified water and let the tea steep for 10 minutes.

When summer arrives we often race into favorite outdoor activities with too much zeal. The next day our body humbly reminds us of our limits. This rescue ritual restores sore muscles and encourages us to take some downtime to rest.

Ask your partner or a friend to give and/or receive a restorative massage with the following clary sage blend—and what could be a better way to enjoy it than outdoors, surrounded by the healing elements of nature?

Outdoor Massage
Select a shady area under a tree or garden pergola to set up your massage table, or place a large blanket on the ground. If you are giving the massage, ask the recipient to lie in a comfortable position and to take three deep diaphragmatic breaths to encourage relaxation. Pour the clary sage blend into your hands and wring together to warm the oil. Gently glide, knead, and wring muscles of affected areas to milk tissues of lactic acid and ease muscle soreness.

CLARY SAGE RECOVERY BLEND

Clary sage is best known for its ability to bring on states of euphoria and for having a narcotic effect on the body. It has a nutty, herbaceous scent that is deeply relaxing, and it is ideal for treating nervous tension and stress-related symptoms. Applied to the body, clary sage has a warming effect, improving circulation to ease lactic acid out of sore muscles. Lavender acts as an antispasmodic while the spicy undertones of bergamot bring a refreshing quality to the blend.

Makes 1 ounce

1-ounce glass bottle

1 ounce carrier massage oil (select one of the carrier oils on pages 40–42)

7 drops clary sage *(Salvia sclarea)* essential oil

2 drops lavender *(Lavandula vera)* essential oil

4 drops bergamot *(Citrus bergamia)* essential oil

Fill the bottle halfway with carrier oil. Add essential oils and shake well. Top off with remaining carrier oil, cover, and agitate a second time. Massage into affected areas.

Special precautions: Avoid using clary sage essential oil if you are pregnant.

For extra-strength muscle relieving blends add 1 ounce of an arnica infused carrier oil (see pages 24–25, 43, and 117). Arnica is a potent anti-inflammatory for the treatment of swelling and joint pain. Or try the stimulating rosemary hot oil infusion (see page 119).

Several years ago I was fortunate enough to be in Provence just before the lavender harvest outside of Grasse. This is the region where most of the lavender is grown for the perfume and food industry and the horizon is filled with a sea of incandescent lavender.

No herb better embodies the spirit of summer than lavender; its long purple spikes are a colorful backdrop to every garden. A hardy perennial, it provides a number of therapeutic uses for the home remedy chest and its aromatic beauty accounts for its popularity in so many cosmetic preparations.

LAVENDER INFUSION BATH

Bathing in lavender, well known for its sedative properties, is a perfect way to reduce stress at the end of a long day. Lavender's sweet, subtle scent calms the overstimulated mind and will help you drift off to sleep. In the nineteenth century lavender waters were commonly administered to women susceptible to "hysteria." Its soothing qualities still hold true.

For use in the bath, first make an infusion by combining ½ cup of the fresh lavender blossoms with 4 cups of boiling water in a French press. Let steep for 20 minutes. Fill bathtub, pour the infusion into the bath, and disappear into the comfort of lavender.

Time-saver tip: If you are too tired to make an infusion from fresh lavender, simply add 5–6 drops of lavender (*Lavandula vera*) essential oil to your bath. It is mild enough to use undiluted in the tub.

LAVENDER WINE

Lavender has an innate ability to ground and soothe anxieties and its steadying power is amplified in this aperitif. Lavender's fortifying properties embolden us to take stock in ourselves to be able to meet life's challenges. Taken internally, lavender tonifies the digestive tract and its antispasmodic properties ease gas pains and digestive spasms.

Makes 4 cups

2–3 cups fresh lavender (*Lavandula vera*) blossoms

2/3 cup sugar

1/2 lemon, thinly sliced

1 quart vodka

Cut leaves and stems off of flowers and place unwashed blossoms into a jar. Add remaining ingredients, stir, and cap. Shake mixture daily and let cure for 2 weeks.

Strain and serve on crushed ice in 1-ounce servings.

During the last century, lavender was used extensively for its antiseptic properties and was commonly diffused into the air at hospitals to act as a disinfectant. This deodorizing powder keeps the skin clean and fresh, while the sweet lavender scent is enlivening. Additionally, this blend can be used to deodorize shoes and perfume bureau drawers. The crisp floral scent is aromatically pleasing sprinkled on fresh bed linens when remaking the bed.

Makes 12 ounces

3/4 cup Bentonite or French white clay

1 cup cornstarch

1/4 cup baking soda

1/4 cup dried lavender buds, finely ground

30–35 drops lavender (*Lavandula vera)* essential oil

In a mixing bowl combine the clay, cornstarch, and baking soda. Using a Cuisinart or mortar and pestle grind the lavender buds to a fine consistency and meld into blend. Add 30–35 drops lavender essential oil (or more if you prefer a stronger scent), and disperse into powder. Transfer to jar or paper container with shaker lid.

A cold water bath for hot, swollen feet provides a refreshing sensation on a summer day. The practice of walking in cold water or cool wet grass was a popular nineteenth-century remedy believed to induce a tonifying reflex action on the organs of the body such as the liver and kidneys. The therapeutic uses of this foot bath include relief for aching feet and for fatigue and exhaustion. The analgesic properties of rosemary will soothe the feet as the woody balsamic scent revives the mind. Tea tree oil is added for its powerful antiseptic ability to deodorize the feet.

Water

1 sprig of rosemary with leaves broken into pieces

6 drops of tea tree essential oil

Fill large bowl or dishpan with cold water. Add rosemary leaves and tea tree essential oil along with a dozen ice cubes. Swish the water to disperse the oil. Dip one foot into water for 30 seconds, remove and rub entire foot vigorously with towel. Return foot to bath and keep repeating the action until foot becomes red. Towel off and dry. Repeat with opposite foot.

GERANIUM IRONING WATER

Legend has it that people used to plant geraniums around their houses because the pungent aroma would help keep evil spirits away. Today the fresh, sublime aroma is a staple of the perfume industry. This is a lovely way to add the soft, rosy green scent of a summer floral to all your clothing and linens. In the summer months let your clothes and bed linens air dry on the clothesline, bringing them indoors when still slightly damp. Add 2–3 capfuls of this ironing water into the steam compartment of your iron and infuse the fabric with the fragrant aroma. Alternatively, place 2–3 capfuls onto a cotton rag or hankerchief and toss with your clothes into the dryer. The uplifting, sumptuous aroma will freshen your wardrobe and linens.

Makes 6 ounces

6-ounce glass bottle
6 ounces distilled water
20 drops geranium essential oil
35 drops lavender essential oil
Coffee filter

Fill the bottle halfway with water. Add essential oils, cover, and shake well. Top off with remaining distilled water, cover, and agitate a second time. Allow mixture to mature for a week and then strain through a coffee filter. Store in a dark glass bottle and shake well before each use.

Hippocrates wrote, "Let thy kitchen be thy apothecary and let foods be your medicine." Using herbs as food adds wonderful flavors to please your palette and imparts medicinal properties through your diet. Most people feel comfortable taking vitamin supplements yet nature provides us with many nutritive allies right in our backyard. This salad has a wide range of therapeutic properties. Fresh dandelion leaves have high amounts of vitamins A, C, and D and are high in iron and potassium. As a digestive bitter, dandelion leaves act as a bile stimulant and laxative and serve as a diuretic to increase the flow of urine. Similarly, parsley contains vitamins A and C, is a potent diuretic to reduce excess water weight, and has a reputation as a breath freshener. Watercress is rich in minerals and vitamin C and adds a distinctive peppery flavor.

Serves 4

1 cup dandelion leaves

1 head Cos, Bibb, or Boston lettuce

1 cup watercress

¼ cup parsley sprigs

¼ cup basil leaves, shredded

Nasturtium flowers (optional)

Salad dressing

Gather fresh dandelion leaves using caution not to pick them near roads or lawns where herbicides, pesticides, or other chemicals might have caused contamination. Wash lettuce and herbs and toss with your favorite salad dressing. Decorate with edible nasturtium flowers for added diuretic effect.

One of the most pleasant ways to enjoy the benefits of herbs is in the bath. Gather a bundle of herbs from your herbal remedy garden selected for their therapeutic and aromatic properties. Include chamomile, an herb with a long history as a nerve sedative and therefore fitting for a soothing restorative bath after a long day outdoors. Chamomile's distinctive applelike scent is very calming mentally and emotionally, good for easing anxiety. Lavender's sedative qualities overlap with those of chamomile and together they will calm frayed nerves or ease dull aches and pains. Add a few sprigs of fresh and uplifting geranium or basil to balance the effect of this bouquet.

Gather all the herbs in a bundle and tie off with a length of cotton ribbon or string. Gently bruise or tear the leaves to release the aromatic oils. Make a loop with the excess ribbon and tie the bouquet underneath the faucet so that water flows over herbs and into the tub. Or, let the bouquet float around you as you relax in the tub.

CITRUS BODY SPLASH

A body splash, also known as an eau de cologne, is an invigorating way to freshen up during the hot days of summer. Pure essential oils have a completely different character than synthetic perfumes and make soft, delicate fragrances that do not overwhelm you when you encounter them. Artificial perfumes can cause allergic reactions and they do not possess the much more delicate and subtle range of tones that genuine essential oils have.

This blend of essential oils is designed to stimulate and refresh but you can create soothing blends as well. Body splashes also provide deodorizing benefits and the vinegar is tonifying.

Makes 6 ounces

Glass jar with lid

10 drops lime *(Citrus aurantifolia)* **essential oil**

10 drops tangerine *(Citrus reticulata)* **essential oil**

5 drops lemon *(Citrus limonum)* **essential oil**

3 drops basil (Ocymum basilicum) essential oil

⅛ ounce vodka

½ ounce white wine or cider vinegar

5 ounces distilled water

Coffee Filter

6-ounce glass bottle

Combine all the essential oils with the vodka in a glass container and shake well. Add vinegar, shake thoroughly, and let rest for 30 minutes. Pour water into the mixture, shake again, and allow mixture to mature for one week. Pour through a coffee filter and store in a glass bottle.

Rosemary, one of the earliest herbs to be recorded for use in medicine, is a superb rejuvenation herb, especially on those days of summer when swaying in the hammock is all you can do to stir up a breeze. Rosemary has a tonifying effect on both the circulatory and the digestive systems, but its main action is on the nervous system, where it acts as a stimulant. Rosemary is traditionally known as a memory enhancer, and legend tells us that Greek students wore rosemary necklaces to improve their concentration. This may prove helpful after you have settled into the hammock and cannot remember where you last saw your crossword puzzle.

Thyme is prized for its antiseptic properties. Combined with lemon, both herbs provide an invigorating tonic guaranteed to pick you up.

Makes 4 cups

3 teaspoons fresh rosemary, separated from stem and broken into small pieces

1 teaspoon fresh thyme

1-inch piece ginger, thinly sliced

1/2 lemon, thinly sliced

4 cups purified water

1/2 cup honey

Place rosemary, thyme, ginger, and lemon in a French press. Add purified hot water and stir. Steep for 10 minutes and strain. Sweeten with honey and serve hot or cold.

Summertime reawakens our sexual yearnings through a will all of its own. Perhaps it is the sensuous feeling of being outdoors with the sun and water on our bodies, or the excitement that comes with walking at night guided by the half-light of the moon and stars. The yin and yang of love is constant, and the human quest for aphrodisiacs speaks to our need to cope with the ebb and flow of sexual desire. Stress is the biggest culprit; if we are run-down from too much work or from staying up too late or from a diet of rich or fast foods we will lose our vitality, which is the essence of sexual energy. In Chinese medicine, the *jing,* or essence of life, is stored in the kidneys, and this essence is the basis of all energy, including sexual energy.

Sexual tonics can be helpful in restoring sexual energy by supporting the kidney and adrenal functions. In general, warming, stimulating herbs are useful for these weak organ functions, in particular, hot and spicy herbs such as cardamom, cinnamon, and clove. You could also try ginger or rosemary to combat exhaustion and fatigue. The following recipe combines American ginseng and licorice root, both containing plant steroids called ginsenosides, as a robust tonic and to support the adrenal system to improve physical stamina. American ginseng is somewhat milder and less stimulating than Siberian ginseng. It gently energizes the central nervous system and helps improve stamina.

Makes 1 cup

½ **teaspoon dried licorice root**

5 **cardamom seeds, crushed**

⅛ **teaspoon cinnamon**

2 **cloves**

1 **star anise**

1 **cup purified water**

20 **drops American ginseng tincture**

Place licorice root, cardamom, cinnamon, cloves, and star anise in a French press. Fill the press to the top with purified boiling water, cover, and let steep for 20 minutes. Strain, pour into cup, and add 20 drops of American ginseng tincture and stir.

Special precautions: Ginseng is not an appropriate remedy for children or pregnant women. Licorice root in large doses can increase blood pressure and may not be appropriate for individuals with hypertension, diabetes, glaucoma, or heart disease.

SENSUAL FEET

The best way to strengthen the libido is to make some time for relaxation. One of the most effective ways to elicit the relaxation response is through massage.

Certain essential oils are known for their aphrodisiac properties. One of the most notable in this category is rose, whose petals were traditionally sprinkled on bridal beds in ancient Rome. Rose's sweet, warm notes appeal to both men and women. This blend combines rose with another ancient aphrodisiac, jasmine. The rich, vanilla-like scent of benzoin and the smoky aroma of sandalwood are calming and relaxing.

The feet have thousands of nerve endings; a soothing foot massage will help encourage relaxation and restore vitality. Using a firm but gentle touch will help win over ticklish feet. Begin by stroking one of your partner's feet with both hands, moving from the toes up to the calves. Next, place both of your hands on top of the foot and gently squeeze the foot first with your left hand then the right. This milking action removes the calcium deposits that accumulate after long hours of standing. While supporting the foot with one hand, try gently stretching the toes and flexing the ankle to loosen the joints. Next, slowly sink your thumb into the bottom of the foot, and using tiny circular movements, locate tender or congested areas. By this point your partner will agree to anything, a guaranteed fire starter.

Makes 1 ounce

1-ounce glass bottle

1 ounce carrier oil (select one of the carrier oils on pages 40–42)

5 drops rose *(Rosa damascena)* **essential oil**

4 drops benzoin *(Styrax benzoin)* **essential oil**

3 drops sandalwood *(Santalum album)* **essential oil**

2 drops jasmine *(Jasminum grandiflorum)* **essential oil**

Fill the bottle halfway with carrier oil. Add essential oils and shake well. Top off with remaining carrier oil, cover, and agitate a second time. Massage into feet or use for full-body massage.

AROMATIC INSECT REPELLENT

Several essential oils act as deterrents for bugs and they are a safe and refreshing alternative to chemical insect repellents. Citronella or lemongrass work beautifully as environmental repellents and should be diffused throughout the room to keep insects at bay. A good remedy for traveling in biting-insect season is to fill your hotel room's bathroom sink with hot water and add a few drops of these oils. As the steam dissipates into the room, the scent will act as a deterrent. To prevent insects from landing on you, a synergistic spray of this recipe will do the trick.

Makes 1 ounce

1-ounce bottle with atomizer

¼ ounce witch hazel

3 drops thyme *(Thymus vulgaris)* **essential oil**

6 drops lemongrass *(Cymbopogon citratus)* **essential oil**

4 drops peppermint *(Mentha piperata)* **essential oil**

¾ ounce water

Pour witch hazel into bottle. Add essential oils, shake well, and top off with water. Screw on atomizer and agitate a second time. Spray directly onto skin or clothing, using caution to avoid the eye area.

Dab a drop of undiluted tea tree *(Melaleuca alternifolia)* essential oil onto bites and stings from mosquitoes, horseflies, spiders, or ticks. The powerful antiseptic properties of tea tree oil will disinfect the area while its warm, camphorous compounds will desensitize the sting. To reduce the swelling and inflammation of bee stings, mix a solution of 1 teaspoon of baking soda, 1 tablespoon of water, and 3 drops of tea tree essential oil in a bowl and apply as a cold compress to the wound.

CHAMOMILE SUN SOOTHER COMPRESS

Despite all the warnings of a diminished ozone layer and the rise of melanoma, people still find the sun irresistible. It is relaxing to feel the sun's rays penetrate the skin; if you do happen to overdo it in the sun, chamomile is an effective remedy to calm overexposed skin. Chamazulene, the main ingredient in German chamomile, is an excellent anti-inflammatory agent and its therapeutic properties are enhanced when used in conjunction with lavender.

3 drops German chamomile *(Matricaria recutita)* **essential oil**

2 drops lavender *(Lavandula vera)* **essential oil**

1 sprig peppermint *(Mentha piperata)* **leaves, gently brusised**

Prepare a cold compress by adding the essential oils and peppermint leaves to a small bowl of ice water. Dip a washcloth into the solution, wring out, and apply to affected areas. Repeat as needed.

Sun, salt, and chlorine take their toll on hair by summer's end. This stimulating blend of essential oils can improve the health of the scalp: avocado oil, fortified with fatty acids, protein, and vitamins A, B, and C, will recondition the shaft of the hair.

Makes ½ ounce

½-ounce glass bottle

½ ounce avocado oil

2 drops tea tree *(Melaleuca alternifolia)* **essential oil**

5 drops rosemary *(Rosmarinus officinalis)* **essential oil**

7 drops bay laurel *(Laurus nobilis)* **essential oil**

Fill bottle halfway with avocado oil. Add essential oils, cover, and shake well. Fill bottle with remaining avocado oil, cover, and agitate a second time.

To apply, wet hair, squeeze out excess water, and towel dry until slightly damp. Pour oil into the palm of your hand and work the mixture into your scalp and through your hair. Massage the scalp with the pads of your fingers for several minutes, working from your forehead to the nape of your neck. Cover your hair with a plastic bag and wrap a towel over the bag to seal in warmth. This allows the oil to penetrate the hair shaft. Leave oil on hair for 20 minutes. Shampoo thoroughly and rinse clean.

5 AUTUMN

AUTUMN

Summer's end arrives with a flurry of activity, a final immersion in all the glory that defines the season, and then suddenly, fall arrives.

The air becomes redolent with the sweet smell of decaying leaves and the smoke of a distant wood-burning stove. Surrounded by the changing leaves and the withering plant life, no other turn of season so clearly defines for us the transitions of life, the passage of time. As the days grow shorter, the darkness ushers us indoors to give us time to rest and reflect, our bodies time to heal. Unfortunately, our current lifestyle tries to thwart this. We receive 20% less sleep than we did 100 years ago, when the average person slept 9½ hours. Our reliance on electrical lighting has changed our normal biorhythms.

Along with the changes in light and the September air that fluctuates between warm and cool, our bodies undergo a transition as well. We can take note of our shifts in energy, our changes of moods, or the flexibility of our muscles and joints. An opportunity appears in autumn to gently push us to observe our patterns and abandon destructive habits or routines. This calls for mindfulness on our behalf so that we do not lose touch with the part of ourselves that is signaling for change.

This turn in seasons with changing temperatures and shifting energy patterns can also make us vulnerable to colds and flu along with fatigue and stress-related conditions. Fortifying yourself with essential oils and herbs that support the immune and adrenal systems will keep you strong and healthy in the months to come. In addition, our skin goes through seasonal changes as it tries to adjust to climate shifts. Using herbs to exfoliate the skin as well as to provide extra moisturizing benefits will help this transition.

As the garden yields its final harvest of vegetables, herbs, and flowers, now is the time to prepare your herbal medicine cabinet to sustain you through the dark months ahead. Simple remedies such as herbal infused oils can be prepared in the fall to help treat a variety of conditions. This is a good time to check your essential oil inventory to ensure that you have a well-rounded supply to remedy a variety of complaints as well as to use for aromatic enjoyment in your home. Don't forget to reorder any carrier oils you may need for blending since these base oils also have therapeutic properties that could be useful as well.

This chapter also explores the healing powers of water. Hydrotherapy has a long history of use by natural health practitioners as an agent of healing. Water can induce deep relaxation and its healing benefits are enhanced when combined with herbs and essential oils.

As the days slowly grow shorter and the evening air becomes crisp and cool, our thoughts reluctantly turn toward the winter ahead. There are several staples for your herbal medicine cabinet that can be prepared in the fall and will prove invaluable in the prevention and treatment of many conditions in the months ahead. Either by harvesting the healing plants in your garden or by visiting your local health food store, you can collect the ingredients to assemble your home remedy chest.

Herbal infused oils are carrier oils that have had herbs steeped in the oil to release their therapeutic properties. Cold infused herbal oils are suitable for flowering herbs such as arnica, calendula, Roman chamomile, and St. John's wort. They are easy to prepare and are an invaluable asset to making bath and massage oils as well as salves. Herbal infused oils are best when made from fresh plants. You can use almost any type of carrier oil as a base but usually the best results come from safflower oil, which absorbs into the skin easily and does not go rancid quickly. The following recipe is for calendula but you can substitute a number of therapeutic herbs from your garden such as arnica, German chamomile, and St. John's wort (see page 43).

CALENDULA INFUSED OIL

Applied externally, calendula, also known as pot marigold, is a wound healer. It is one of the most effective remedies to treat dry or aggravated skin conditions such as eczema or dermatitis. Use the blend as a base oil in your massage oils for dry skin or for the healing of burns and scars. Its sweet honey-like aroma is aromatically pleasing.

Makes 1 quart

Two 1-quart canning jars
Calendula *(Calendula officinalis)*
   flower heads to fill 2 jars
16 ounces safflower oil
Cheesecloth or muslin bag

Harvest the calendula flower heads on a sunny day and discard any soiled parts of the plant. Do not wash the flower heads as the water will encourage mold to grow. Using your hands, gently bruise or break the flowers to extract as much active plant material as possible. Densely pack the entire canning jar with calendula flower heads and cover completely with oil to the rim of the jar. Place lid tightly on jar, label with the name of the plant and the date, and leave in a sunny windowsill or greenhouse for 2–3 weeks. Using a cheesecloth or muslin bag, strain the mixture into a container. Now repeat the process by densely packing another canning jar with bruised calendula flower tops and fill to the brim with the once-infused oil. Cap the jar and let steep for an additional 2–3 weeks. Strain the mixture once again through a piece of cheesecloth or muslin bag and store in a colored glass bottle.

The therapeutic properties of the leaves of herbs are most easily extracted by heating the material in the carrier oil. This is also a good method if the plant material you are working with is dried rather than fresh. The camphorous, stimulating qualities of rosemary make it a valuable infused oil to invigorate the nervous and digestive system as well as to soothe muscular aches and pains. If kept in a cool, dark place, infused oils will last up to a year and can be used alone or blended with other herbal and essential oils for massage and bath oils. Try warming the oil and massaging it in a clockwise direction into the abdomen to relieve constipation or rub it into sore muscles to ease stiffness.

Makes 1 quart

2 cups fresh rosemary leaves

16 ounces safflower oil

Heatproof glass bowl or
   double boiler

Cheesecloth or muslin bag

Gently bruise or break the rosemary leaves to extract as much active plant material as possible. Put the oil and the rosemary in the glass bowl and place over a pan of simmering water or double boiler. Gently heat the mixture for 2 hours and then strain through cheesecloth or muslin bag into a measuring cup to cool. Store oil in a glass bottle.

Floral Waters

Floral waters are lightly scented waters that can be used to freshen or hydrate the skin. Although they are not as potent as hydrosols, which are the genuine waters left over from the distillation of essential oils, floral waters are great to use on long plane rides or in over-heated apartments to aromatically rehydrate the skin. With an atomizer, you can spray them directly onto your skin or pour a capful onto a cotton pad and wipe your face. Floral waters are easy to use as a makeup remover and are beneficial for toning the skin after cleansing. They are also useful as aromatic base materials in making cosmetic preparations. Try using lavender, rose geranium, or neroli floral waters to delicately refresh your skin.

Makes 4 ounces

4-ounce glass bottle

4 ounces distilled water

30–40 drops of essential oil

Coffee filter

Fill the bottle halfway with water. Add essential oils, cover, and shake well. Top off bottle with water, cover, and agitate a second time. Allow mixture to mature for a month and then strain liquid through a coffee filter. Store in dark-colored glass bottle.

Ruby Grapefruit Exfoliating Paste

In the fall, skin tone becomes rough and uneven as dead skin cells are sloughed off from our summer tan. This stimulating body scrub is actually a salt glow made with coarse sea salt and invigorating essential oils. It will leave your skin feeling smooth and polished. Grapefruit is a favorite essential oil because its delicious uplifting fragrance induces a feeling of euphoria and is a great reviver. It is terrific to use in skin care because it stimulates circulation at the skin's surface, bringing radiance and tone.

Massage this paste vigorously over the entire body in the bath to enhance circulation and stimulate the sebaceous glands. It will act as a rubefacient and will bring a pink glow to the skin, leaving you feeling refreshed and revitalized.

Makes 4 ounces

Glass bowl

4-ounce glass jar

1½ ounces almond oil

25 drops grapefruit
(*Citrus paradisi*) essential oil

6 drops lavender (*Lavandula vera*)
essential oil

10 drops lime (*Citrus limetta*)

14 drops tangerine (*Citrus reticulata*)
essential oil

3 ounces coarse sea salt

Combine almond oil and essential oils in a glass jar and shake vigorously to disperse the oils. Pour mixture into a glass bowl and add the sea salts a little at a time, stirring until you have a thick paste; let sit for 1 hour. Pour into glass jar. This paste will last for up to 6 months if covered and stored in a dark glass container.

Special precautions: This is a very stimulating treatment and should not be used by individuals with sensitive or inflamed skin. Do not use if skin lesions are present.

For people with sedentary work lives, there are many benefits to working out. But for a lot of us, exercise is pure drudgery. The media and the fitness industry have had their effect on us: many people don't feel healthy if they don't look toned and buff. Yet exercise regimens have become complicated with elaborate equipment and costly gym memberships. And if an exercise routine is boring or too complicated or takes too much time, it will be abandoned.

Exercise helps us maintain a certain body weight and improves cardiovascular function by keeping arteries clear of debris and cholesterol levels down. It boosts the immune system, and perspiration helps to eliminate toxins. Vigorous exercise stimulates endorphin production, which acts as a natural opiate to calm our stress-filled bodies and creates a sense of well-being.

Walking is a simple method of reaping all the benefits of exercise without joining a gym or occupying too much of your time. By walking vigorously for 45 minutes at least five times a week you can stay in shape and enjoy the beauty of the outdoors. The great thing about walking is that it releases you of feeling burdened by the exercise routine. It can be a lot easier to motivate yourself to get out of bed in the morning and simply take a walk than it is to convince yourself to go to the gym. There's no equipment needed (other than a decent pair of sneakers) and it's easy to fit into your day.

On a deeper level, walking can provide another type of meditation practice, especially for individuals who find sitting meditation too difficult. Walking provides us with another opportunity to establish a sense of connection with ourselves and to sharpen our awareness skills with each step we take. Just as with sitting meditation, walking meditation requires that you focus the mind and be present with each step. As distracting thoughts try to pull you away, stay focused on the mechanics of walking—the sensation of the foot as it touches the ground, your shifting weight and your breath. Allow your awareness to be completely focused on the moment. Notice how your body relaxes in movement as the mind grows still.

SPICE SYNERGY

The pungent, aromatic essence of autumn is one of my favorite sensory pleasures with the ripe, sweet mulch of decaying leaves coming from the earth. This is a time for reflection and new beginnings, a new sense of purpose. As the weather cools, enjoy the warmth of the indoors, staying inside and cocooning.

This synergy combines both grounding and stimulating essential oils to focus the mind and energize you on a subliminal level. The sweet, balsamic notes of vanilla calm the mind and combined with the rich, resinous tones of sandalwood and vetivert will promote deepening meditative states while the spicy, sharp scent of cardamom will enhance clarity of thought.

Makes 4 ounces

4-ounce glass bottle

4 ounces water

15 drops sandalwood *(Santalum album)* **essential oil**

12 drops vetivert *(Vetiveria zizanoides)* **essential oil**

8 drops vanilla *(Vanilla planifolia)* **essential oil**

3 drops cardamom *(Ellettaria cardamomum)* **essential oil**

Fill the bottle halfway with water. Add essential oils, cover, and shake well. Top off bottle with water, cover, and agitate a second time. To dispense, pour 2 tablespoons of synergy into top of diffuser. Shake well before dispensing.

Special precautions: Sandalwood, vetivert, and vanilla are all thick, resinous essential oils. Do not use this synergy in an electric diffuser or vaporizer as it will clog the nebulizer.

Rich in vitamin C, iron, and an abundance of other minerals, burdock root has a good reputation as a blood purifier and has strong diuretic properties, helping promote the elimination of toxins via the kidneys. Nourishing burdock root will provide optimum nutrition to the immune system to keep you healthy and strong during the cooler months. As an added bonus, burdock is prized as a valuable tonic for clear skin. This delicate salad has a crisp texture and lots of added zing from the fresh ginger.

Makes 2 servings

½ **burdock** *(Arctium lappa)* **root**
   (2 cups)

1 **carrot (½ cup)**

1 **tablespoon fresh ginger**

½ **cup vegetable soup stock**
   (can be made from vegetable
   bouillon cubes)

3 **tablespoons soy sauce**

2 **teaspoons marin (Japanese**
   rice vinegar)

1 **tablespoon sake**

Sesame seeds (optional)

Cut the burdock root, carrot, and ginger into thin matchstick slices and place in a pan with soup stock. Simmer for 4–5 minutes. Add the soy, marin, and sake and simmer for an additional minute. Remove from heat, sprinkle with sesame seeds, and let sit until cool. Serve at room temperature.

This recipe was developed by Carin Houck-Wylie, a Naturopathica staff member, during one fall season when all of us were succumbing to the flu. Ginger has been used as a culinary spice and medicine for thousands of years. Native to tropical Asia and cultivated commercially in the West Indies and Africa, ginger has warm, fiery properties that help to combat winter chills and ward off colds and flu. This effect is enhanced by the properties of lemon, loaded with vitamin C. Echinacea, or purple coneflower, was prized by Native Americans for its healing qualities and was known to treat a variety of ailments from snakebites to fever. In Europe, natural healers have long valued the benefits of echinacea as an immune system stimulant, and recent scientific studies by the Commission E in Germany have validated its effectiveness. Good-quality echinacea leaves a slight tingling sensation on your tongue.

Makes 2 quarts

2 quarts purified water

6 organic fresh lemons (medium sized)

3 tablespoons fresh ginger, peeled and grated

2/3 cup honey

20 drops echinacea (Echinacea purpurea) root tincture

In a large pot, bring the water to a boil. Juice the lemons using a fork and discard the seeds. Add the lemon juice and pulp to the water. Fold in the peeled, grated ginger. Let boil gently for five minutes, then turn down the heat and add the honey. Cover and simmer for an additional minute. Remove from stove, pour into a cup, add 20 drops of echinacea, and stir. Enjoy hot or cold. Drink this brew 4 times a day at the first sign of infection for sore throats, colds, and flu.

If the sea is our true ancestral home, perhaps the ritual of soaking in an aromatic bath or luxuriating in a steaming shower is about more than cleansing the body. The healing power of water induces in us a deep sense of relaxation and well-being as we metaphorically wash away our stress and anxiety; it soothes the soul.

Bathing has been considered vital to emotional and physiological health since antiquity. Hippocrates prescribed the way to health by means of an aromatic bath and scented massage every day. The ancient Greeks built great bath halls, and the Romans constructed elaborate baths of marble and gold for the aristocracy and the warrior class to fortify themselves—often at natural mineral hot springs.

Two eighteenth-century Austrians, Vincent Preissnitz and later, Sebastian Kneipp, laid the foundation for modern water therapy. Their ideas on the therapeutic use of water included alternating hot and cold water treatments, herbal and steam baths and compresses, as well as careful attention to the temperature of the water and the duration of treatments—all in order to strengthen the natural defense systems of the body. These specific regimens are still practiced today at most European spas. The mineral content of the baths is scrutinized for therapeutic properties and administered internally and externally.

The benefits of water therapies are many and their outcomes usually dependent upon two factors: the temperature of the water and the length of immersion. Further benefit is derived if herbs and essential oils are added to the treatment. Warm water is a sedative, promotes perspiration, and acts as an analgesic and antispasmodic for aches and pains. Cold water acts as a restorative tonic to boost energy. Alternating hot water with short bursts of cold water is excellent for circulation, moving toxins out of the tissues. Hydrotherapy can also include various kinds of steam inhalation treatments and compresses.

YLANG YLANG CALMING BATH OIL

This rich, exotic bath oil helps when you are overtired or overstimulated and need to unwind at the end of a long day. Ylang ylang is cultivated in East Asia, where in Malay dialect its name means "flower of flowers." A sweet, spicy floral, its effect is that of a harmonizer, calming anxious thoughts to elicit peace of mind. The soft, luscious scent of rose and the intoxicating vanilla-like scent of benzoin enhance ylang ylang's soothing effect.

Makes 4 ounces

4-ounce glass bottle

4 ounces carrier oil (select one of the carrier oils on pages 40–42)

6 drops ylang ylang *(Cananga odorata)* **essential oil**

8 drops rose otto *(Rosa damascena)* **essential oil**

12 drops benzoin *(Styrax benzoin)* **essential oil**

Fill the bottle halfway with carrier oil. Add essential oils and shake well. Top off with remaining carrier oil, cover, and agitate a second time. Add 2–3 capfuls to warm bath and soak in tub for 20–30 minutes to sedate and relax the body.

JUNIPER AND LEMON SHOWER OIL

This is a hot and cold water treatment designed to invigorate and tone the body. By alternating the temperature of the water you dilate and constrict the blood vessels, creating a pumping action that is excellent for circulation, counteracting muscle fatigue for the entire body while locally stimulating circulation to help minimize the buildup of lactic acid in the tissues. This treatment is especially useful when you know you have overstretched your limits at the gym or on the tennis court.

Stand under the hot spray of your shower for 5 minutes. Follow immediately with a cold spray for 5–30 seconds. The effect of the cold water will be sedating if the duration is less than 10 seconds and rejuvenating and toning if longer than 10 seconds. Return to the hot spray and repeat the cycle.

This refreshing juniper and lemon oil will help revitalize the tissues, acting as an excellent restorative for stiff muscles and joints. Just before finishing your shower, add 5–6 drops of the blend to a washcloth and rub all over (taking care to avoid the eyes). The woody, balsamic scent will invigorate your mind.

Makes 1 ounce

1-ounce plastic bottle

1 ounce carrier oil (select one of the carrier oils on page 40–42)

7 drops juniper *(Juniperus communis)* **essential oil**

3 drops lemon *(Citrus limonum)* **essential oil**

4 drops grapefruit *(Citrus paradisi)* **essential oil**

Fill the bottle halfway with carrier oil. Add essential oils and shake well. Top off with remaining carrier oil, cover, and agitate a second time.

{*autumn*

The benefits of herbs and essential oils can be enhanced by the use of compresses. This technique consists of a wet cloth soaked in hot or cold water and applied to the body to sedate or stimulate an area. Compresses can be made of terry cloth, cotton, or flannel and should be large enough so that they can be folded several times to help retain heat or cold. A cold compress inhibits circulation and is useful when applied to sprained ankles or bruises to help control inflammation. A hot compress, also called a fomentation, is a muscle relaxant and is useful when applied for menstrual or stomach cramps or sore muscles.

The spicy, slightly nutty scent of marjoram is soothing and calming to the mind, and the herb possesses antispasmodic properties to ease cramping. You can use the following recipe as a stomach compress for indigestion, in particular for symptoms of bloating or a rumbling stomach, or to ease the pain of menstrual cramps.

Fill a large pot or dishpan with warm water, add 2–3 drops of marjoram essential oil, and swish water to disperse the oil. Heat a kettle of water on the stove and place nearby to keep the temperature of the compress bath constant. Fold the compress cloth into three parts and dip the center into hot water. Wring out the ends and apply to affected area. To minimize heat loss, cover the compress with a wool blanket. Resoak the compress in bath as soon as it loses heat.

EVERLAST REGENERATING FACE SERUM

Everlast, also known as *immortelle,* has an excellent reputation for healing wounds. This essential oil is invaluable in regenerative skin care, in particular for scar tissue. Everlast soothes dry and inflamed skin conditions and is especially helpful for mature and sun damaged skin when used with other regenerative oils such as frankincense. Together the two have a tonic effect on the skin and help to slow down the appearance of wrinkles. The carrier oil in this blend consists primarily of jojoba, a lightweight oil similar to our skin's natural oil. Rose hip seed oil, fortified with gamma linolenic acid, promotes cellular repair.

Makes 1 ounce

1-ounce glass bottle

3/4 ounce jojoba oil

3 drops everlast
(Helichrysum italicum) essential oil

5 drops frankincense (Boswellia
carteri) essential oil

3 drops rose (Rosa damascena)
essential oil

3 drops sandalwood (Santalum
album) essential oil

1/4 ounce rose hip seed oil

Fill the bottle partway with jojoba oil. Add essential oils, cover, and shake well. Top off bottle with rose hip seed oil, cover, and agitate a second time. To use, apply 3–4 drops to moist cotton pad and wipe over entire face. For added benefit use in conjunction with floral waters (see page 120) and burdock root tincture (see page 57).

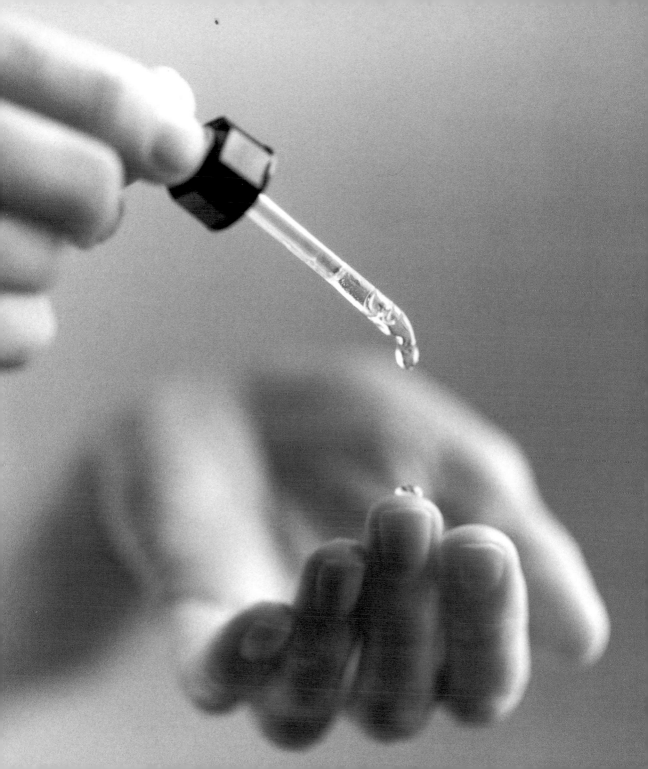

WINTER

The cold of winter keeps us indoors, where our bodies resonate with the stillness outside.
Though this is a good time to turn inward and rest, our modern lifestyle does not tend to allow for the art of contemplation—and yet this is what nature seems to be telling us to do. The long nights provide fertile ground for our creativity as well as our need to rest, if only we will yield to our instincts.

This chapter begins by focusing on self-care rituals that reestablish a sense of connection to ourselves. All this requires is being a good observer. Begin in the morning when you wake up. Did you allow yourself enough time to sleep and do you feel rested? How does your body react when you drink coffee in the morning? Notice how you feel after eating certain types of food—does it leave you energized or lethargic? If it is the latter, perhaps your diet is too rich and you need to learn to appreciate simple foods. If mood swings are a problem, pay attention to what sets them off. Is it the weather or because you need to spend more time nourishing yourself? A complete inventory—listening to the messages your body is sending you, rather than avoiding them—is the first step to establishing a healthier lifestyle.

Wise natural healers understand that good health is not simply the absence of sickness. Some alternative therapies are extreme in the view that good health is achieved only through adhering to strict rules geared toward "detoxifying" the body, that the body is riddled with toxins, parasites, and even bad thoughts that must be purged through fasting, strict diets, colon therapy, excessive exercise, and a mountain of vitamins and supplements to bring the body back into "balance" and to avoid ever being sick. But the common cold reveals our body's innate cleansing healing mechanism, and we should honor this process rather than fear it, because it may teach us something. Perhaps we have been pushing too hard; staying at home forces us to rest. A cold or flu can make us feel miserable but there are many natural health care rituals that can ease the discomfort.

This chapter will focus on ways to nourish the different systems of the body— immune, nervous, digestive, circulatory, and respiratory—as they undergo change. The healing benefits of nutritious foods that build strength and vitality will be explored, as well as specific recipes that combat common winter maladies such as depression, fatigue, dry skin, and colds and flus, to name a few.

SOOTHING FACE MILK

Winter skin care revolves mainly around keeping the skin hydrated. Itching or peeling skin over a wide area such as your cheeks or chin indicate dryness while localized flaky patches can be signs of a stress-related dermatitis. To soothe the skin, cut down on cleansing. Overcleansing strips the skin of its protective barrier of natural oils, making it more vulnerable to cold and wind. Use a mild cleanser free of synthetic detergents and alternate it with an antiseptic or calming floral water such as lavender or chamomile (see page 120). Spritz the floral water onto your face to remove makeup or to tone the face.

Dehydrated skin can also be soothed with a nutritious oat milk bath. The high concentrations of salicylic acid in oats can calm aggravated skin conditions and will relieve itching from dermatitis. Oat milk is deeply emollient to the face, leaving the skin soft and moisturized.

Place 1/2 cup of oats into a washcloth and fasten closed with a rubber band. Fill bathroom sink with hot water and soak the washcloth for 5 minutes. Squeeze washcloth several times to release oat milk and apply to your face as a compress. As water cools, splash oat water onto your face for soft, silky skin.

It is troubling how divorced from our bodies we let ourselves become, as if we exist only from the shoulders on up; when a friend suddenly reaches over and kneads our back we moan with pleasure as tension is released. Far from being a machine, the physical body needs to be nurtured. Try to interrupt the need to always be on the go and set some time aside to check in with how you are feeling.

One way to do this is with a body scan. Begin by lying on the floor using blankets or cushions to get in a comfortable position. This meditation is easy to do because it requires less effort than a seated position. Begin by taking a few minutes to focus on your breath, taking deep, full breaths as you extend the diaphragm to the floor of the abdomen. As you exhale, let go of any tension you may be holding in your chest. You will get a bigger release if you make a sighing noise as you exhale.

After a few minutes, begin to scan your body. Bring your attention to tense areas, breathe into them, and exhale any muscle tension or anxiety. As the floor supports your body, you can completely let your muscles go and allow your body to sink into deep relaxation. You can scan the body in a linear pattern, starting from your toes to the top of your head, or you can move about the body in a free-form fashion, moving from one constricted area to the next, gradually letting go. Let your feet dangle apart and feel your calves and thighs get heavy. Relax the pelvis. Let your lower spine sink into the floor and allow the rib cage to expand as your breathing becomes slow and easy. Feel your shoulders sink toward the floor as your neck gently lengthens. As the body slowly unwinds, listen to any sensations or feelings that may surface. This deep state of relaxation allows you the opportunity to reconnect with unconscious feelings; using your breath to calm any anxieties that may surface will make it easier to face them. You can do this exercise for 20–30 minutes in the morning or in the evening before bedtime to see how your body is feeling day to day.

R O O T V E G E T A B L E S O U P

Root vegetables such as carrots, beets, and turnips are fortified with vitamins and minerals and are a good way to replenish your body in the winter when it may be lacking some of these essential elements. Excessive amounts of coffee, alcohol, and rich food as well as insufficient amounts of water can deplete the body. When many other vegetables are out of season, winter root vegetables are bursting with beneficial nutrients.

Makes 6 servings

6 medium-size or 3 large leeks, white
    part only, cleaned and sliced
2 small onions, chopped
1 to 2 garlic cloves, to taste,
    minced or pressed
2 medium carrots, peeled
    and chopped
1 celery rib, chopped
2 small turnips, peeled and diced
1 1/2 pounds potatoes (russet or
    waxy), peeled and diced
6 cups water, vegetable stock,
    or chicken stock
Bouquet garni made with a
    bay leaf and 2 sprigs each
    thyme and parsley
Salt and freshly ground pepper
    to taste

1 cup milk as needed
2 to 4 tablespoons dry white wine
    or sherry (optional)
Drained nonfat yogurt or
    crème fraîche for garnish
Chopped fresh parsley for garnish

Combine vegetables, water or stock, and bouquet garni and bring to a boil. Add salt, reduce heat, cover, and simmer 1 hour. Remove bouquet garni and puree soup through the medium blade of a food mill, or with a hand blender. Do not use a food processor or blender, or soup will be too smooth. Return to the heat and thin with milk as desired. Add salt and pepper to taste. Stir in the wine if desired. Serve, garnishing each bowl with a dollop of yogurt or crème fraîche and a sprinkling of parsley.

VITABOLIC GREENS

Dark leafy greens are a good source of fiber and provide an excellent supply of vitamins and minerals. Many types of leafy vegetables, especially kale, collard greens, and beet greens, are rich in beta carotene due to their high chlorophyll content as well as vitamin C. Both of these agents act to protect against cancer. These leafy greens are at their seasonal peak from January to April. This simple recipe of tender and delicious kale, collard greens, and beet greens will leave you feeling strong and energized. By cooking them quickly you will help to preserve their nutrients.

Makes 2 servings

1 teaspoon sesame seeds
1 cup kale greens, chopped
1 cup collard greens, chopped
1 cup beet greens, chopped
1 tablespoon extra virgin olive oil
1 clove garlic, peeled and pressed
1 lemon, halved and de-seeded

Toast sesame seeds in a small saucepan on top of the stove over medium heat until seeds begin to turn light brown, about 3 minutes. Set aside. Trim away any tough stems and soak greens in water and rinse thoroughly. Pour olive oil into a wok or large, heavy-bottomed skillet and turn heat on medium-high. When pan is hot (not so hot that the oil starts to smoke) add garlic and still-damp greens and squeeze half a lemon over them. Stir constantly and squeeze other half of lemon onto greens to avoid burning. Quickly sauté greens until just tender. Remove from heat and sprinkle with toasted sesame seeds.

Sleep is as essential as food, water, and oxygen to the body. During sleep, our nervous system gets a chance to rest and the body moves into an anabolic state in which energy conservation, cellular repair, and growth processes take over. Over a hundred years ago, the term "midnight" meant just that—the middle of a night's sleep. But for many of us midnight is when we head off to bed. Chronic lack of sleep reduces our resistance to infection, affects our ability to concentrate, and makes us emotionally vulnerable or volatile.

Many people do not experience the natural rhythms of sleep and suffer from insomnia or disrupted sleep, caused by physiological and emotional factors. It helps to develop good sleeping habits. Be aware of your diet. Avoid stimulants such as coffee and soda and try to eat light meals at night at least two hours before bedtime. Exercise helps promote sleep especially if your job requires you to sit behind a desk all day. Try to empty your mind at night. Sketch out a list of all the things you have to do and the things that you are worrying about, to stop them from running through your mind, so you can rest peacefully. Not watching the late evening news or reading the newspaper helps in this regard.

CALMING CHAMOMILE BATH

Chamomile was well known to the ancient Greeks, who likened its scent to apples; hence the name *chamaimelon*, "earth apples." Its sedative properties have been used for centuries to treat insomnia and anxiety. In this blend, sweet, fresh Roman chamomile is used for its calming, slightly narcotic qualities. Combined with soothing lavender, hypnotic rose, and a touch of refreshing bergamot, this is your lullaby to dreamland.

Makes 1 ounce

1-ounce glass bottle

1 ounce carrier oil (select one of the carrier oils on pages 40–42)

2 drops Roman chamomile *(Anthemis nobilis)* essential oil

3 drops lavender *(Lavandula vera)* essential oil

4 drops rose otto *(Rosa damascena)* essential oil

3 drops bergamot *(Citrus bergamia)* essential oil

Fill the bottle halfway with carrier oil and add essential oils. Cover and shake well. Fill with remaining carrier oil. Cover and agitate a second time. Pour 2–3 capfuls into still bath water and disperse with hand. Soak in tub for 20–30 minutes and relax.

Special precautions: Chamomile can cause dermatitis in some individuals.

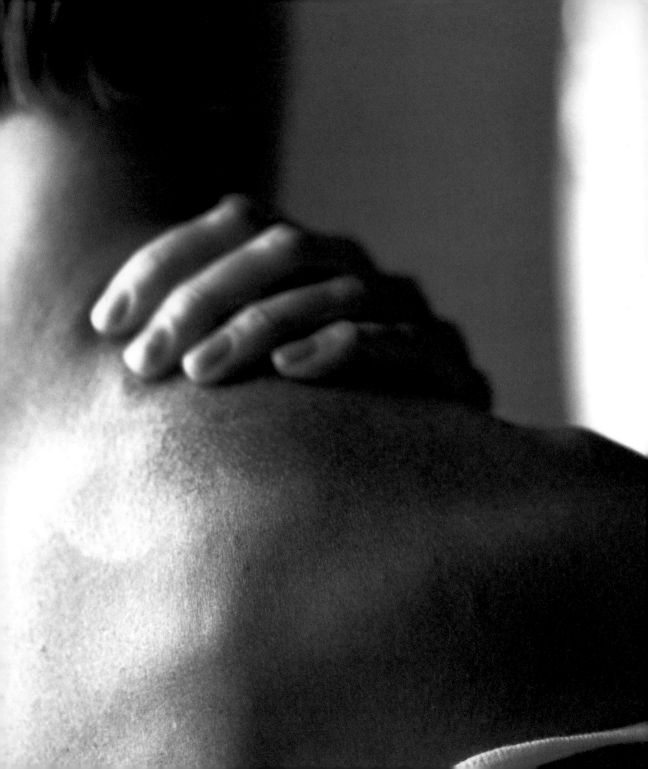

Soothing touch and the therapeutic properties of essential oils relax physical and emotional tension. Of all the aromatics, sandalwood has the longest tradition of being used in religious rituals. Its deep, sweet, balsamic scent is powerfully grounding to the mind. This exquisite oil is an effective nighttime treatment for anxiety and insomnia since it induces deep meditative states. Keep this blend next to your bed as a rescue remedy for sleep.

Makes 1 ounce

1-ounce glass bottle with dropper
1 ounce carrier oil (see page 40–42)
10–12 drops sandalwood
   (Santalum album) **essential oil**

Fill bottle halfway with carrier oil and add sandalwood essential oil. Cover and shake well. Fill with remaining carrier oil, cover, and agitate a second time. Squeeze one dropper of oil into the palm of your hand, gently wring hands together, and hold over your nose and eyes. Inhale deeply 3 times. Massage oil into your temples and rub firmly over outer ear. In traditional Chinese medicine, the ear possesses many acupressure points relating to the gall bladder meridian, which regulates stress levels. Gently massage the back of the neck and shoulders using a circular movement with the pads of your fingertips. Place your fingers on your cheeks and massage your jaw line to relax the muscles that move your mouth up and down. Next, using one hand at a time, massage the pectoral muscles of the chest using your fingertips. Everyone holds a lot of emotional tension in the chest and abdomen and massaging these areas will help facilitate the nervous system to let go. Be sure to work the spaces in between the ribs as these intercostal muscles hold a lot of tension. End your session with a quick wringing of the feet to bring fresh blood to stiff toes and joints.

ARNICA MUSCLE AND JOINT RELIEF

There's nothing so humbling as the cold, damp chill of winter to remind us that we are getting older. Our bones ache, our joints get stiff, and our muscles seem to strain much more easily. Arnica is a toxic herb when taken internally but is an effective external remedy for rheumatic pain and muscle stiffness. It eases swelling and is perfect for muscle aches and sprains. Marjoram, well known for its analgesic and antispasmodic effects, is a good complement to arnica. Marjoram was reputed to increase longevity; its sweet, peppery aroma is inviting at this time of year and its warming qualities soothe aches and pains and calm the restless mind.

Makes 4 ounces

4-ounce glass bottle

1 ounce arnica infused herbal oil (see pages 24–25, 43, and 117)

1 ounce grapeseed oil

26 drops marjoram *(Origanum majorana)* essential oil

5 drops Roman chamomile *(Anthemis nobilis)* essential oil

4 drops lavender *(Lavandula vera)* essential oil

5 drops cardamom *(Elletaria cardamomum)* essential oil

2 ounces almond oil

Fill bottle partway with arnica infused herbal oil and grapeseed carrier oil. Add essential oils and shake well. Top off with almond carrier oil, cover, and agitate a second time. Apply to affected areas as needed.

This potent green tea is a blend of matcha powder and sencha leaves. Matcha powder is used in tea ceremonies in Japan. The pungent powder is whipped with a bamboo whisk into a frothy tea and served in carefully prescribed rituals of mindful practice where the art of making tea is an act of meditation. The ritual originated in China during the Song Dynasty (960–1280). Taoist monks heated tea leaves and compressed them to form a cake. This was then made into a powdered form with a mortar and pestle. Powder tea, often served with fragrant flowers, became immensely popular. Taoists proclaimed it to be an elixir of immortality. A Zen Buddhist monk named Eisai is credited with introducing the use of matcha tea in temple rituals in Japan.

Matsuchiri-sencha tea is a combination of the basic sencha green tea leaf blended with the powdered matcha. This blend is a much more potent form of green tea; since the matcha is in powdered form, you actually ingest particles of the leaf. The high chlorophyll content is iron-rich and the catechins help protect against cancer and heart disease. Matsuchiri-sencha tea has a soft, mellow flavor. It makes a delicious wintertime beverage and a nutritive elixir.

Makes 1 cup

1 cup purified water

1 teaspoon matsuchiri-sencha tea

Bring water to a gentle boil and pour over tea. Steep for 30–60 seconds. Strain. You can reuse the leaves for your second cup of tea as the taste improves with each infusion of water.

SOOTHING BALANCE TONIC

It seems that no matter how we try to take care of ourselves during the winter months we are always susceptible to a bout of the winter blues. With no sign of spring, the short days and long nights make people prone to symptoms of depression and lack of energy. Craving starchy foods and indulging in meals that are high in fat to keep us warm, many people gain weight. This, in turn, heightens feelings of depression. Although severe depression is caused by an imbalance of brain chemicals, many people suffer from situational depression and anxiety stemming from emotional difficulties or life transitions.

Removing all stimulant foods—such as coffee, chocolate, soda, and sugar—from the diet will help ease anxiety, as will increased exercise. This soothing tonic contains a blend of herbs that are well known for their tranquilizing effect to ease stress and tension. Kava kava root and skullcap are both sedative herbs that renew the central nervous system.

Makes 1 cup

1 cup purified water

½ teaspoon dried peppermint
(Mentha piperita) leaves

½ teaspoon dried German chamomile
(Matricaria recutita)

1½ teaspoons dried skullcap
(Scutellaria lateriflora) leaves

20 drops St. John's wort (Hypericum
perforatum) tincture

20 drops kava kava (Piper
methysticum) tincture

Bring water to a boil and pour over peppermint, chamomile, and skullcap. Steep for 5 minutes. Strain and add 20 drops each of St. John's wort and kava kava and stir. Drink twice a day.

Special precautions: If you are on prescription antidepressants, you should establish a working relationship with a health care practitioner or doctor trained in herbal medicine. Herbs can be used to ease off of prescription antidepressants but only with a qualified practitioner.

Garlic is a powerful natural medicine whose health benefits have been recorded since ancient times. The Egyptians are said to have fed it to their slaves to keep up their strength for building the pyramids, and Roman soldiers ate it to increase endurance. Today, research points to garlic's ability to lower cholesterol and reduce clotting in the blood. Garlic is well known to enhance the immune system, a favored home remedy to reach for at the first sign of a cold or flu. Raw garlic contains the strongest antibiotic properties; heat from cooking destroys some its therapeutic effects. This recipe retains garlic's robust flavor and antiviral properties and it won't give you bad breath. It is a savory variation of the traditional onion soup and is easy to prepare. Onions, also a member of the *Allium* family, mirror the cholesterol lowering benefits of garlic.

Makes 6 cups

6 cups vegetable stock (can be made from vegetable bouillon cubes)

2 medium sized potatoes, peeled and cut into chunks

3/4 teaspoon salt

1 teaspoon dried thyme

2 cups chopped onions

2 tablespoons olive oil

8–10 large cloves garlic, peeled and minced

2–3 tablespoons minced fresh parsley

Bring 6 cups of vegetable stock to a boil in a medium saucepan and add the potatoes, salt, and thyme. Simmer for 20–30 minutes until potatoes are tender. In a separate saucepan, sauté the onions in olive oil until translucent. Add the onions and the garlic to the vegetable stock and simmer for five minutes. Ladle half of the mixture into a blender or food processor, puree until smooth, return to the pan, and stir. Serve garnished with minced parsley.

BREATHE EASY DECONGESTANT

Bathing in tea tree essential oil at the very first sign of a sore throat or stuffy nose can often stop a cold from developing. The antiviral properties of tea tree oil have a long history of use by the aborigines of Australia, where most tea tree oil is produced. Eucalyptus and tea tree oil are both recognized for clearing congested sinuses and soothing inflamed mucous membranes. This bath, with its camphor aroma, brings the healing gift of the Australian forests.

Makes 1 ounce

1-ounce glass bottle

1 ounce carrier oil (try a sedative Roman chamomile herbal infused oil, see page 43)

3 drops tea tree oil *(Melaleuca alternifolia)* **essential oil**

8 drops eucalyptus *(eucalyptus globulus)* **essential oil**

2 drops thyme *(Thymus vulgaris linalool)* **essential oil**

Fill bottle halfway with carrier or herbal infused oil and add essential oils. Cover and shake well. Fill with remaining carrier oil, cover, and agitate a second time. Pour 2–3 capfuls into still bath water and disperse with hand. Soak in tub for 20–30 minutes and relax.

In ancient Greece and Rome, to earn a crown of laurel leaves was a high honor. Bay laurel has always been a popular culinary herb as well. It has a reputation as a remedy for digestive complaints, especially loss of appetite. Bay laurel also works preventatively to ward off colds and flu. In this spicy blend, its warming and sedative effects create a soothing ambiance when diffused in the air. Thyme, proven to have antiseptic and antiviral properties, works synergistically to help you stay healthy. Keep this spray next to your bed. When home with a cold or flu, mist your linens and bedroom to keep bacteria away and to pick up your spirits.

Makes 4 ounces

4-ounce glass bottle with atomizer

4 ounces distilled water

30 drops bay laurel
   (Laurus nobilis) essential oil

10 drops eucalyptus (Eucalyptus globulus) essential oil

8 drops thyme (Thymus vulgaris linalool) essential oil

Fill the bottle halfway with water. Add essential oils, cover, and shake well. Top off bottle with water, twist on atomizer, and agitate a second time. Shake well before using.

Steam inhalations are a simple and very effective form of treatment to ease congestion. The hardy perennial thyme is a powerful antiseptic and was traditionally used to purify the home and to preserve meats and other foods. Thymol, the primary active ingredient, is used in many over-the-counter remedies. Thyme is particularly effective in treating colds and respiratory infections; besides fighting infections, its expectorant qualities clear phlegm from the lungs. In this inhalation remedy, peppermint will also help open nasal passages and sinuses.

Heat a kettle of water on the stove and keep nearby to add extra heat to your inhalation. Pull a chair up to the bathroom sink and stack several pillows on the chair for a comfortable seat. Fill the clean basin with hot tap water, add 3 drops of thyme oil and 2 drops of peppermint oil, and swish water with hand to disperse the essential oils. Cover head and shoulders with a towel and lean over the basin, making a tent to hold in the steam and volatile oils. Breathe deeply for 5 minutes, inhaling through the nose. Add more hot water from the kettle to raise the temperature as needed.

CHAMOMILE FACE SERUM

Chamazulene, the active ingredient in German chamomile, gives this essential oil its characteristic deep blue color and is responsible for its anti-inflammatory benefits.

During the colder months, this serum is one of the most effective remedies to calm rosacia or almost any type of dry, itchy skin condition. The soothing properties of chamomile will have a calming effect on the emotional level as well. This is important since most skin imbalances have their roots in emotional stress and not just an external irritant. Evening primrose oil has a reputation as a healing agent for scars and is added to this blend to promote tissue repair along with avocado oil, which is rich in fatty acids.

Makes ¹/₂ ounce

¹/₂-**ounce glass bottle**

¹/₄ **ounce evening primrose oil**

3 drops German chamomile
   (*Matricaria recutita*) essential oil

6 drops neroli *(Citrus aurantium)*
   essential oil

4 drops lavender *(Lavandula vera)*
   essential oil

¹/₄ **ounce avocado oil**

Fill the bottle halfway with evening primrose oil. Add essential oils and shake well. Top off with avocado oil, cover, and agitate a second time. Apply to affected areas.

Juniper has long been known for its detoxifying properties. In the nineteenth century, sprigs of juniper and rosemary were burned in French hospital wards as a disinfectant. Juniper is a diuretic. It helps tone the kidneys to stimulate elimination and after a night of overindulgence, juniper will help clear the body of toxins. Grapefruit is added for its uplifting effect on the emotions and to quell nausea while lavender relaxes the overburdened nervous system.

Makes 4 ounces

4-ounce glass bottle

4 ounces carrier oil (select one of the carrier oils on pages 40–42)

22 drops of juniper *(Juniperus communis)* **essential oil**

28 drops of grapefruit *(Citrus paradisi)* **essential oil**

8 drops of lavender *(Lavandula vera)* **essential oil**

Fill the bottle halfway with carrier oil. Add essential oils and shake well. Top off with remaining carrier oil, cover, and agitate a second time. Add 2–3 capfuls to warm bath and soak in tub for 20–30 minutes to sedate and relax the body.

PURIFYING SYNERGY

During the winter months we are easily susceptible to colds and flu: respiratory infections such as bronchitis can linger on for weeks. The best defense is to keep the immune system strong with plenty of rest along with a healthy diet and nutritive herbs. Diffusing essential oils in the home is also beneficial, especially since many essential oils have antibacterial properties to keep germs at bay. This blend uses the powerful antiseptic properties of eucalyptus, thyme, and lemon to disinfect the home and strengthen the body's resistance to disease.

Makes 4 ounces

4-ounce glass bottle

4 ounces purified water

24 drops eucalyptus *(Eucalyptus globulus)* essential oil

15 drops lemon *(Citrus limonum)* essential oil

5 drops thyme *(Thymus vulgaris)* essential oil

Fill the bottle halfway with water. Add essential oils, cover, and shake well. Top off bottle with water, cover, and agitate a second time. To dispense, pour 2 tablespoons of synergy into top of diffuser. Shake well before dispensing.

Most of the recipes in this book use simple household ingredients or can easily be found on a trip to the grocery, hardware, or health food store. The following database will provide you with a list of companies that can easily provide raw materials through mail order as well as a list of organizations and educational opportunities to learn more about natural healing.

Mail-Order Sources for Herbal Remedies

Avena Botanicals
219 Mill Street
Rockport, ME 04856
(207) 594-0694

High-quality dried herbs and tinctures, oils, salves. Catalog.

Blessed Herbs
109 Barre Plains Road
Oakham, MA 01068
(508) 882-3839

Excellent source of quality dried bulk herbs and tinctures. Catalog.

Fragrant Earth
2000 Second Avenue, Suite #206
Seattle, WA 98121
(800) 260-7401

High-quality essential oils and aromatherapy raw materials. Catalog.

Naturopathica
74 Montauk Highway
East Hampton, NY 11937
(800) 669-7618
www.naturopathica.com

Premium essential oils, infused herbal and carrier oils, herbal teas, tinctures, natural remedies, botanical skin care. Catalog.

Original Swiss Aromatics
P.O. Box 6723
San Rafael, CA 94903
(415) 479-9121

Comprehensive selection of genuine essential oils.

Trinity Herbs
P.O. Box 100
Graton, CA 95444
(707) 824-2040
Dried herbs, beeswax, teas.

Bottles and Jars

SKS Bottle & Packaging
3 Knabner Road
Mechanicville, NY 12118
(518) 899-7488

Supplier of amber and cobalt glass bottles as well as plastic and metal containers. Catalog.

Sunburst Bottle Company
5710 Auburn Boulevard #7
Sacramento, CA 95841
(916) 348-5576

Wide selection of plastic and glass bottles and containers. Catalog.

Organizations

American Association of Naturopathic
Physicians
601 Valley Street, Suite 105
Seattle, WA 98109
(206) 298-0126
www.naturopathic.org

*Provides referrals to accredited or licensed
naturopathic physicians in your area.*

American Botanical Council
P.O. Box 144345
Austin, TX 78714
(512) 926-4900

*Nonprofit educational organization focused on
the uses of herbs and phytomedicines.
Publishes* Herbalgram, *a quarterly magazine
dedicated to increasing consumer awareness
about herbs.*

American Massage Therapy Association
820 Davis Street, Suite 100
Evanston, Il 60201
(708) 864-0123

*Educational organization that promotes the
massage therapy profession. Good referral
source for certified massage therapists in your
area.*

National Association for Holistic
Aromatherapy (NAHA)
836 Hanley Industrial Court
St. Louis, MO 63144
(888) ASK-NAHA

*Professional aromatherapy organization found-
ed to promote educational guidelines for the
aromatherapy profession as well as a resource
of suppliers and practitioners. Publishes*
Scentsitivity, *a quarterly aromatherapy jour-
nal.*

Education

The Australasian College of Herbal Studies
P.O. Box 57
Lake Oswego, OR 97034
(800) 487-8839
E-mail: achs@herbed.com

*Correspondence courses in aromatherapy and
herbal medicine.*

Esalen Institute
Big Sur, CA 93920
(831) 667-3000

*Educational center with workshops on mas-
sage, yoga, meditation, and mind-body connection.*

The Institute of Dynamic Aromatherapy
2000 Second Avenue, Suite 206
Seattle, WA 98121
(800) 260-7401
www.fragrantearth.com

Aromatherapy certification and workshops.

Jeannie Rose
Aromatic Plant Project
219 Carl Street
San Francisco, CA 94117
(415) 564-6785
E-mail: hydrosol@excite.com

Aromatherapy certification and workshops.

martha-rose-shulman.com

A Web site devoted to healthy cuisine.

Pacific Institute of Aromatherapy
P.O. Box 6723
San Rafael, CA 94903
(415) 479-9121

Aromatherapy certification.

References

Barasch, Marc Ian. *The Healing Path*. New York: Penguin Books, 1993.

Berube, Robert. *Evolutionary Traditions: Unique Approaches to Lymphatic Drainage & Circulatory Massage Techniques*. Hudson, NH: Robert Berube, 1988.

Buchman, Dian Dincin. *The Complete Book of Water Therapy*. New Canaan, CT: Keats Publishing Inc., 1994.

Haas, Elson M. *Staying Healthy with Nutrition: The Complete Guide to Diet and Nutritional Medicine*. Berkeley, CA: Celestial Arts, 1992.

Hoffmann, David. *The New Holistic Herbal*. London: Element Books, 1990.

———. *The Complete Illustrated Holistic Herbal*. London: Element Books, 1996.

Lawless, Julia. *The Illustrated Encyclopedia of Essential Oils*. London: Element Books, 1995.

Nhat Hanh, Thich. *The Miracle of Mindfulness: A Manual on Meditation*. Boston: Beacon Press, 1987.

———. *Peace Is Every Step: The Path of Mindfulness in Everyday Life*. New York: Bantam, 1991.

Ody, Penelope. *Home Herbal*. London: Dorling Kindersley Ltd., 1994.

Podreka, Tomislav. *Serendipitea*. New York: William Morrow & Co., 1998.

Price, Shirley. *Practical Aromatherapy*. London: Thorsons, 1993.

Ryman, Danielle. *The Aromatherapy Handbook*. New York: Bantam Books, 1991.

Schnaubelt, Kurt. *Advanced Aromatherapy*. Rochester, VT: Healing Arts Press, 1998.

———. *Medical Aromatherapy: Healing with Essential Oils*. Berkeley, CA: Frog, Ltd., c/o North Atlantic Books, 1999.

Shealy, Normon C. *The Complete Family Guide to Alternative Medicine*. London: Element Books, 1996.

Shulman, Martha Rose. *Light Basics Cookbook*. New York: William Morrow & Co., 1999.

———. *Mediterranean Light*. New York: Bantam Books, 1989.

Tierra, Michael. *The Way of Herbs*. New York: Simon & Schuster Inc., 1980.

Tisserand, Robert. *The Art of Aromatherapy*. Essex: C.W. Daniel, 1985.

Weed, Susan S. *Healing Wise*. New York: Ash Tree Publishing, 1989.

Weil, Andrew. *Natural Health, Natural Medicine*. New York: Houghton Mifflin Co., 1998.

———. *Spontaneous Healing: How to Discover and Enhance Your Body's Natural Ability to Heal Itself*. New York: Alfred A. Knopf, 1995.

Worwood, V.A. *The Fragrant Pharmacy*. London: Macmillan, 1990.

Kabot-Zinn, Jon. *Wherever You Go, There You Are*. New York: Hyperion, 1994.

Index